# THE POWER OF GOOD NEWS

# THE
# POWER OF
# GOOD
# NEWS

Feeding Your Mind with
What's Good for Your Heart

## HAL URBAN

BK®

Berrett–Koehler Publishers, Inc.

Berrett-Koehler Publishers, Inc.
1333 Broadway, Suite 1000
Oakland, CA 94612-1921
Tel: (510) 817-2277
Fax: (510) 817-2278
www.bkconnection.com

ORDERING INFORMATION

**Quantity sales.** Special discounts are available on quantity purchases by corporations, associations, and others. For details, contact the "Special Sales Department" at the Berrett-Koehler address above.

**Individual sales.** Berrett-Koehler publications are available through most bookstores. They can also be ordered directly from Berrett-Koehler: Tel: (800) 929-2929; Fax: (802) 864-7626; www.bkconnection.com.

**Orders for college textbook / course adoption use.** Please contact Berrett-Koehler: Tel: (800) 929-2929; Fax: (802) 864-7626.

Distributed to the U.S. trade and internationally by Penguin Random House Publisher Services.

Berrett-Koehler and the BK logo are registered trademarks of Berrett-Koehler Publishers, Inc.

Printed in the United States of America

Berrett-Koehler books are printed on long-lasting acid-free paper. When it is available, we choose paper that has been manufactured by environmentally responsible processes. These may include using trees grown in sustainable forests, incorporating recycled paper, minimizing chlorine in bleaching, or recycling the energy produced at the paper mill.

Cataloging-in-Publication Data is available at the Library of Congress.
Library of Congress Control Number: 2021930310
ISBN: 978-1-5230-9278-9

First Edition
27  26  25  24  23  22  21          10 9 8 7 6 5 4 3 2 1

Produced by Wilsted & Taylor Publishing Services
Copyediting: Nancy Evans | Text design: Nancy Koerner
Cover design: Susan Malikowski, DesignLeaf Studio

Dedicated, with much love and thankfulness, to my Alpha Delta Gamma brothers and to two honorary sisters at the University of San Francisco, for sixty-plus years of friendship, support, laughs—and good news.

| | | |
|---|---|---|
| Mike Anthony | Jerry Crowe | Peter Lombardo |
| Peter Brekhus | Howard De Nike | Dick McGregor |
| Sandy Brekhus | Rick Fischer | Tom McBrearty |
| Lee Brossier | Bud Grandsaert | Ron Menhennet |
| Cathy Brossier | Chris Gray | Ray Pariani |
| Jim Brovelli | Ron Howson | Doug Taylor |
| Ming Chin | Patrick Lawing | David Woolsey |

There is nothing on this earth more to be prized than true friendship.

—Thomas Aquinas (1225-1274)

With every news alert or breaking story, our world seems to be pushed further and further into crisis. It is taking a serious toll on our environment but also on our mental health.

—Alexandra Pattillo
CNN health reporter

Being exposed to positive information benefits us emotionally, physically, and mentally. It can contribute in a meaningful way to a happier and healthier life.

—Tal Ben-Shahar, PhD
Harvard psychologist

# Contents

# Preface

We're going to spend quite a bit of time together in these pages, so you should know a few things about me. It will help if you know what influenced me growing up and what changed me later.

### Raised in a Negative Environment

I grew up in a small town in Northern California. My dad was a good man in many ways. He was conscientious, worked hard, and was generous with his time, building talents, and money. But, like all of us, he had some flaws. I think they stemmed from his grueling childhood. Born in 1910, the son of two recent immigrants from Lithuania, he grew up as the oldest of eight children on a farm in Oregon. Because he went to work on the farm at age five and was also responsible for helping with his younger siblings, he had little time for an education. He left the farm as a young man and moved to San Francisco to become an ironworker.

Unfortunately, my dad was negative, angry, loud, confrontational, and he swore a lot. Most men of his generation didn't communicate well and rarely talked about their feelings or expressed affection. My dad never told me he loved me or was proud of me. I never had even one meaningful conversation with him. This was the environment I was raised in. The angry words and lack of affectionate words left their mark on me. It took a long time to recover. For the record, my dad *did* love me and *was* proud of me—he just couldn't tell me. He did a lot of things for me later that proved it, and I will appreciate those acts forever.

You may be wondering about the role of my mom. In the 1940s and '50s when I was growing up, she, like most women, played a traditional role. She stayed home with the kids, cleaned the house, did laundry, shopped, cooked, and played a subservient role to the man of the house. My mom was actually one of the sweetest, kindest, and most giving persons I've ever known. She had a great influence on me, but not until later.

## A Life Changed by Teachers

Things began to improve when I got to high school, where, for the first time, I had good male role models. My best teachers in both high school and college were positive, caring, and supportive. They helped me learn to forgive my dad and realize my potential for a better life. I wanted to be like them, guiding young people in the right direction. I wanted to be a teacher.

Dr. Tom McSweeney, a wonderful education professor, said, "The first thing successful teachers do is form good relationships with their students. If you can reach 'em, you can teach 'em." That became my career mantra. He added what has become an educational proverb: Kids don't care how much you know until they know how much you care.

During all thirty-six years of my teaching in high school and university, I devoted the first few classes to connecting—getting to know my students and helping them get to know me and one another. As corny as it may sound, my first goal was to turn my classroom into a caring community. I learned early on that good teaching involves more than academics. It's also a highly personal and social endeavor.

## The Teacher Becomes an Author

A few years after getting settled in my teaching career, I was still fighting some demons from my youth: anger, negativity, and resentment. A friend and colleague turned me on to the writings of Og Mandino. Then came Napoleon Hill, Denis Waitley, John W. Gardner, Abraham Maslow, and Carl Rogers. Their books had a profoundly positive effect on my thinking, and the demons began their exit. I had my first post-college realization that what you feed your mind comes out in your life. I still revisit these books on a regular basis.

These authors, and those who followed, had such a positive impact on me that I began to wonder why our schools didn't teach more about the importance of good character. We were doing a good job of teaching academics, but we weren't helping our students learn about life in the real world. This thinking led to my first book, *Life's Greatest Lessons*, which in a nutshell is about the essentials of a good life that I wanted to pass on to my three sons and my students. Writing became an extension of my teaching. I try to connect with my readers in the same way I did with my students: with meaningful stories, valuable life lessons, and a little humor.

Another author who influenced me was William Zinsser, who at the time was a brilliant professor at Yale. In *On Writing Well*, his suggestion that writing is a personal transaction jumped off the page at me because of my teaching style. He also says that a writer should be part entertainer, another thing a teacher has to be. He advises authors to "express the warm and loveable person you are." Well, here I am, folks. I just hope that when someone asks if you like this book, you'll say, "Do I ever! And the author is so warm and loveable."

I share more of my personal story in the second chapter of this book, which is about discovering the power and joy of sharing good news. The richness comes, not from me, but from the people who taught me along the way, including my high school students. One day during our current events time, they suggested that we focus as much on good news as on the bad news that we get from the media. That simple but brilliant suggestion planted the seed for this book.

I'm writing this as if I were talking to you one-to-one, teaching a class, or speaking to a friendly audience. I consider each of these to be highly personal ventures. I hope you read this book as if a trusted friend were passing on some of his best advice. That suggestion may also sound a little corny, but it's straight from this teacher's heart. Enjoy!

A writer
is obviously at his more
natural and relaxed when
he writes in the first person.
Writing is, after all,
a personal transaction
between two people.

**—William Zinsser**
**(1922-2015)**

# Introduction

## Three Reasons for Writing This Book

### 1. To show how good news
### contributes to our well-being

One of the great rewards of writing is learning, especially when it's about improving mental health. In preparing to write this book, in addition to the joy of reading factual stories of progress and acts of charity and kindness, I discovered numerous research projects that help us understand the many benefits of positive mental input. Positive input can be good news, an uplifting story, a sincere compliment, unexpected contact with a dear friend, or a simple expression of thankfulness. These studies, covered in chapter 5, make the strong case that this kind of input promotes good health—physical, mental, emotional, psychological, and spiritual.

### 2. To point out that the good in
### the world far outweighs the bad

I choose to focus on the good for a simple reason: there's far more good in the world and in people than there is bad. This is a *fact*, not a foolishly optimistic pipe dream, and it's been established over and over by solid research. I'm an ardent admirer of the people who have proven, and continue to prove, that many significant aspects of life have been steadily improving for many years. I try to summarize their key findings in chapter 4, along with letting you know where you can find the original source of this uplifting truth.

### 3. To offer a few suggestions for adding and spreading more joy in your life

I don't have any secrets or magic, as many book titles claim to do, to either make you happy all the time or vastly improve the world. But I do have a few suggestions worth passing on. During my many years of learning, I've picked up some simple strategies for dealing with, even rising above, some of the harsh realities that life deals out. My strategies aren't based on scientific research or intellectual theory, but on the best kind of learning—in the school of life —and are simple, common-sense things we can do to see the good, appreciate life more, and make the

Consuming positive news can lead to increased acceptance of others, a feeling of community, and motivation to contribute to social change.

—Jodie Jackson
Constructive
Journalism Project

most of each day that we're given. The key is to do these things on a regular basis. None of them requires a major time commitment. There's no one-system-fits-all. I'm just throwing out some ideas that you might want to try.

## Three Key Points

### 1. This book is not about ignoring the bad news.

I have a positive outlook on life. It's the result of forming the daily habit of feeding my mind with positive information and training my brain to look for the good. However, I don't ignore bad news or advise anyone else to ignore it. In fact, I strongly recommend that people stay well informed for two reasons: it makes us better citizens and it helps keep us safe.

Please understand also that I'm not in any way trying to diminish the severity of the horrors, losses, injustices, and anguish felt so deeply by thousands of people in our recent history. Their pain is real. It's also a wake-up call for our current leaders and the rest of us to work toward needed reforms, especially in furthering our country's founding principle of liberty and justice for all.

### 2. This book is not about being happy all the time.

I'm all for happiness, but the simple truth is that no one can be happy all the time, no matter how hard you try. One of the main points I wanted to make when I wrote my first book, *Life's Greatest Lessons*, back in 1990, was "Life is hard, and not always fair." Nothing in the past thirty years has changed my mind.

Unfortunately, pain and suffering are part of all of our lives. We can't escape, ignore, or make this reality go away. But we can learn effective ways to deal with it, even to rise above it. That's what this book *is* about. As the famous philosopher Friedrich Nietzsche taught us, "That which does not kill us makes us stronger."

### 3. This book is not a response to all the bad news of 2020.

It would be logical for you to think that I wrote this book because of COVID-19 and all the other bad news of 2020 and beyond. But that's not the case. I started writing it in the relative calm of 2019, and its roots go back much further. I've felt for many years that the media report only on the negative side of life and that the other side needs more exposure. I'm not alone—smart and influential people are working on this issue now, and I'm hopeful that things will improve.

> On every level I feel there is a weird disconnect between the way the world is presented to us in the media and the way it really is.
>
> —**Malcolm Gladwell**

Let me ask you, my readers, as I often asked my students: What gets your attention? What are you letting in? Is it toxic or nourishing?

*Attention to negative things equals negative emotions.*
*Attention to positive things equals positive emotions.*

—JENNICE VILHAUER, PHD
*Psychology Today*

Dr. Jennice Vilhauer pinpoints the main intent of my questions in two sentences: "Attention to negative things equals negative emotions. Attention to positive things equals positive emotions." I fervently hope that this book helps you pay more attention to those positive things that give you a lift and help you see more of the good around you.

### Yin and Yang: The Dark and Bright Sides of Life

The yin-yang symbol of the universe and life comes from ancient China and has been traced back to the fourteenth century BCE. The earliest records date back to the Shang (also called Yin) dynasty (1600–1046 BCE). The symbol greatly influenced both Taoism and Confucianism and is universally accepted today as a representation of the duality of nature—two halves that come together to represent the whole. Yin, the dark side, and yang, the bright side, refer to the balance of life. With the bad comes the good, and with the good comes the bad.

Pain, suffering, death, crime, corruption, violence, racial injustice, poverty, economic disparity, natural

## MY DEFINITIONS

| | |
|---|---|
| GOOD NEWS | Anything you see, hear, or read that makes you feel good. This includes seeing people you like (even pictures of them or seeing their names) and anything that makes you laugh. |
| INPUT | Information going into your mind, whether put there by someone else or chosen by you. |
| HEALTH | Physical, mental, emotional, and social well-being—a resource for living a full life. |
| HAPPINESS | A state of well-being and satisfaction with life, or at least with the direction it's going in. Happiness does not mean the absence of pain and suffering, which is impossible. Being healthy, being thankful, always learning, and enjoying positive social relationships are major components of happiness. |

disasters, and any other negative you can think of make up the yin. These sorrows are the primary focus of the news media.

Health, happiness, progress, achievement, success, justice, opportunity, natural beauty, kindness, honesty, adventure, charity, entertainment, sports, and every positive you can think of make up the yang. These joys are also part of our world. But they're *not* the primary focus of the news media.

It would be a shame to ignore all the good going on around us. Recognizing it has been proven to improve our moods, our health, and our well-being. The good news is that a number of committed people want to challenge the news industry to present a more balanced picture of the world. You'll find some of them and their organizations in the section "Sources for More Good News" at the end of this book.

In the meantime, I hope you'll join me in finding the good, appreciating it, and passing it on.

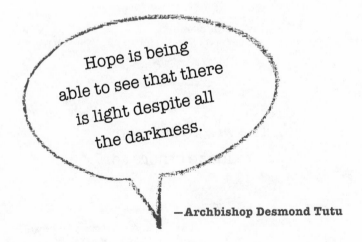

Hope is being able to see that there is light despite all the darkness.

—Archbishop Desmond Tutu

## A Few Words of Wisdom on Happiness

Even a happy life cannot be without a measure of darkness, and the word happy would lose its meaning if it were not balanced by sadness.

—Carl Jung
(1875-1961)

Happiness is not a goal; it is a by-product.

—Eleanor Roosevelt
(1884-1962)

The way to be happy is to make others so.

—Robert Green Ingersoll
(1833-1899)

You become happy by living
a life that means something.
I suspect the happiest people you know
are the ones who work at being kind,
helpful, and reliable, and happiness
sneaks into their lives while doing
those things.

—Rabbi Harold Kushner

Happiness is when
what you think,
what you say,
and what you do
are in harmony.

—Mahatma Gandhi
(1869-1948)

# THE POWER OF GOOD NEWS

The care and feeding
of the mind is just as important
as the care and feeding
of the body.

—Mortimer Adler (1902-2001)
Philosopher and author

## CHAPTER 1

# Wake-Up Call

*You are what you feed your mind*

### An Aha! Moment about Feeding the Mind

I was in my early thirties when I began reading books about personal development. A colleague who read similar books asked me if I'd heard of Zig Ziglar. I thought he was kidding and had made up the name. But I learned that Zig Ziglar, from Yazoo City, Mississippi, was a real person from a real place.

My friend said Ziglar would be speaking in Oakland in a few days and urged me to check him out. Then I saw an ad in our local paper about "A Day with Zig." I needed a lift, so I bought a ticket and called in sick for the next day (teachers call this a mental health day). I was looking to "renew and rejuvenate" myself, as the ad promised.

Early the next morning I drove to Oakland and managed to land a front-row seat. Hoping for an uplifting experience, I got far more. That day turned out to be one of the most meaningful of my life—what the great psychologist Abraham Maslow called a peak experience, one that changed my thinking, feelings, and life.

Zig opened the day by making jokes about his name, about Yazoo City, and about some of his stumbles earlier in life. He had amazing charisma, and I was hooked, mostly because he seemed so genuine. His main theme was that we can vastly improve the quality of our lives, even during hard times, if we can learn to change our thinking. His workshop wasn't about positive attitude or positive thinking or positive mindset or positive outlook or positive anything. He said firmly that he was 100 percent in favor of all of those. Then he added, "But they don't just happen." He emphasized that no one can give them to us, and that we can't will them into ourselves. The most important point of the day, the one he wanted us to go home thinking about for the next several days, was

> *You are what you are because*
> *of what goes into your mind.*

Zig hesitated after saying this, knowing that most of us were writing it down. He asked, "How many of you have heard that statement before?" No hands went up. "How many of you would like to know more about it?" All the hands went up. He said, "Let me ask you a few more questions that might help you get a better grasp of my main point."

- **Would you allow someone carrying a 50-pound bag of trash to dump it in your living room?**
  The room was silent for a few minutes. He wanted us to think about it and form some mental images. I was

wondering why he asked such a no-brainer question. Then came the next one.

- **Do you allow anyone to dump trash into your mind?**
  This was my Aha! moment. The guy next to me said, "I had never thought of that. I guess a lot of crap *does* get dumped into our minds every day. I better start paying closer attention." I was thinking exactly the same thing. And I've paid much closer attention ever since. That defining moment led to the better care and feeding of my mind. It also had an immensely positive effect on my teaching.

### Three More Questions

Zig broke us into small groups and asked us to answer and discuss three more questions, which are just as relevant today as they were in back the early 1970s.

### 1. How much information goes into your mind during an average day?

This question was hard to answer then and is even harder to answer today. But thanks to neuroscientists who have a bent for research, we have some credible answers. If we translate "bits of information" into language, we take in well over 100,000 words per day (or 34 gigabytes, if you prefer tech terms). That comes out to about 220 book pages. This amount was much less in the disco-loving, non-tech 1970s.

In our current hi-tech world, we get peppered daily with a wide array of sounds, words, and images. It's no wonder that social psychologists tell us we're on sensory overload, as our eyes, ears, and minds are bombarded with increasing frequency. The good news is that we have effective ways to keep much of the trash out.

### 2. Who or what is feeding your mind?

Then: The main sources of information in the 1970s were newspapers, magazines, books, radio, TV, news media, family, friends, colleagues, faith and social groups, and various other organizations.

Now: All of the above are still with us, but their levels of influence have significantly changed. In addition, we've added the Tech Big Five: computers, Internet/email, websites/blogs, smart phones/tablets, and social media. With them has come an increasing explosion of information.

Please don't get me wrong. I'm not saying any of these sources of information are bad. I use all of them extensively, and deeply appreciate each. But I also keep in mind that there's a dark (yin) side to everything. A constant stream of horrible crimes and unspeakable cruelty is available on the Internet, which gives us another good reason to look for the yang.

### 3. Is the information healthy or unhealthy?

Zig pointed out that some of our input is neither positive nor negative. It's simply information we need to function on a daily basis, such as getting directions. He said, "Let's focus on those messages we receive that evoke strong feelings, the ones that lift us up or drag us down. How can we take in more of the healthy and less of the unhealthy?"

The group I was in agreed that Zig had increased our

awareness of the huge number of messages we were receiving, the sources and intent of those messages, how they affected us, and, most important, that we needed to take more control over what goes in to our minds, and what shouldn't go in. That was the theme of the day, as it is the theme of this book.

Zig closed this part of the workshop by distributing what looked like a postcard. He suggested we read the card frequently and give serious thought to our answers. I did exactly that, and it resulted in a significantly positive change in what I was feeding my mind. It was a simple, helpful, and powerful instrument. I hope you'll try it.

**You are what you are because of what goes into your mind.**

1. Who/what puts the most information into your mind?

2. How much time do you spend with each source?

3. Which ones are healthy? Which ones are unhealthy?

4. Are you able to eliminate any of the unhealthy input?

5. Are you able to increase the amount of healthy input?

6. What are five sources you can go to for healthy input?

**You can change who you are by changing what goes into your mind.**

## Wrapping Up with Zig

At the end of the day I got in line to meet Zig and buy his book *See You at the Top*. Since the books were at the back of the room, and I was at the front, I ended up last in line. That turned out to be a bonus. When I finally got to Zig, he smiled and said, "I see they saved the best for last. Welcome, my friend." I thought he would be tired and anxious to get away, but he made me feel like the most important person in his life. Great leaders do that.

He asked what I did for a living. When I told him I was a teacher, he lit up even more. "The toughest job in the world," he said, then hesitated and added, "and the most important." I was starting to love the guy. He went on to explain that he had always admired his relatives who were teachers because of their dedication, caring, and hard work. "What I do is way easier than what they do," he added. I thought he was joking, but about twenty years later I became a speaker, and it dawned on me that what he had said about speaking being easier than teaching was the absolute truth.

Zig asked me what stood out during the workshop. I told him that I had come needing a lift and had received a bigger one than I had hoped for. I added that the opening session on what we feed our minds was of the most value because that was a question I had never given much thought to. He smiled and said, "I hear that a lot. What goes in between the ears has a way of coming out in our lives. We say or do things as the result of our thoughts, and our thoughts come from what our minds are fed. Our minds are blank tablets when we're born, but they start getting filled in pretty quickly, for good or for bad. Oh, how I wish more people understood this, and that they taught it in school." I assured him that I would do my best to pass on his teaching to my students, which I did for the rest of my career. Not only did my students hear, "You are what you are because of what goes into your mind," they saw it in writing in big letters every time they came into my room. I'm a big believer in visible reminders, so I had a sign made and put it up in front of the room. I explained it to my students, told them about my day with Zig, and assured them I would do my best to put only positive and helpful information into their minds. The big reminder on the wall helped.

## Two Modern-Day Examples of
## What Goes into a Mind Comes Out in a Life

*Example #1. A child becomes a terrorist*

This extreme example is a sad one, but it's real. It shows us what happens when a young mind is constantly filled with negative and hateful messages. The United Nations Office on Drugs and Crime (UNODC) put out a booklet in 2017 titled *Handbook on Children Recruited and Exploited by Terror-ist and Violent Extremist Groups*. It explains the techniques used by terrorists, particularly indoctrination, often called brainwashing, that lead to children turning into monsters. If they're enslaved, exposed to constant fear, and told over and over that people of other races, other religious beliefs, and other cultures are evil and must be destroyed, they start moving in that direction. The more times you hear something, especially when you're young, the more likely you are to believe it and act on it. These children become what they are because of what goes into their minds.

*Example #2. An angry child grows kinder*

My friend Jenny is a loving and dedicated fourth-grade teacher in Virginia. Several years ago, she got a new student, named Billy, who was major trouble right from the start. He was angry, at times withdrawn and at times boisterous; he hit other kids, yelled, and generally disobeyed.

Jenny looked into his record and learned that Billy had just been taken from his home because of verbal and physical abuse, neglect, and unsanitary living conditions. Both of his parents had serious drug problems. He had been told from the beginning that he was worthless, stupid, and would never amount to anything. What had been going into his mind was coming out in his life.

The school social worker, the principal, Jenny, and two caring foster parents, all working together, changed the direction of Billy's life within a year. How? With love, kind words, encouragement, praise, and every positive experience they could provide for him. He entered a new world in which he was told that he was important, capable, and good—new environment, new messages, new person. Billy is now grown, married, a father of two, and an award-winning teacher. He became who he is today because five loving people changed what was going into his mind.

### Choosing Your Input

"You were given a free will—the power and freedom to make choices. What you do with it will determine the quality of your life." I learned this in my first college philosophy class when I was seventeen. It stuck. It became a foundational piece of my life as an individual, a father, a teacher, and an author. "We live by choice, not by chance" is the title of an early chapter in *Life's Greatest Lessons*. The concept also appears in all my other books, so it's no surprise that it fits in this one as well.

If we are what we are because of what goes into our minds, then it's in our best interest to choose positive, healthy, and uplifting input whenever possible. From that input come our beliefs, values, and being. You are what you are because of what goes into your mind.

> The greatest power that a person possesses is the power to choose.
>
> —J. Martin Kohe
> Psychologist,
> author

Granted, we can't choose *all* of it. We can't choose what other people say, what we hear at work and at social gatherings, or the images we see throughout the day. But by increasing the awareness of our power to choose, we *can* screen out much of the harmful and let in more of the helpful.

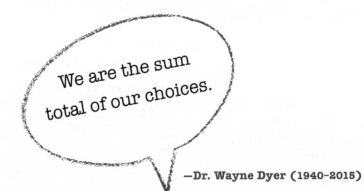

We are the sum
total of our choices.

—Dr. Wayne Dyer (1940-2015)

Every day stand guard
at the door of your mind.

—Jim Rohn (1930-2009)

The mind grows by what it feeds on.

—J. G. Holland (1819-1881)

It is the food which you furnish to your mind that will determine the whole character of your life.

—Emmet Fox (1886-1951)

Our "good news time" has really had a positive impact on my life. I see the world differently and appreciate things a lot more now. It's something I'll take with me when I graduate.

—Shannon Sealey
High school student, 1982

I did "good news time" every morning with my employees for more than 30 years. We started every day in a good frame of mind and with positive energy. So simple, yet so powerful.

—Shannon Sealey Barnes
Retired real estate executive, 2019

## CHAPTER 2

# What My Students Taught Me

*The power and joy
of sharing good news*

### A Teacher's Dumb Luck Leads
### to a Life-Changing Discovery

Lesson planning, or preparing for class, is one of the most important and demanding aspects of teaching at any level. If you're a teacher, you know exactly what I mean. If you're not, you'd probably be surprised at how many hours it requires.

Most of the time, the better prepared you are, the better the class goes. But on occasion, a lesson plan you thought would be great totally bombs—every teacher's biggest nightmare. And on other occasions, you might get just plain lucky. That's what this next story is about: dumb luck that turned into something positive, life-changing, and long-lasting for my students and for me. It's a joy to share it with you.

Let's start with a definition: *Dumb luck* is defined by the *Macmillan Dictionary* as "the way in which something good happens completely by chance, without being planned or deserved." That's what happened way back in the late 1960s, in the early days of my career. My dumb luck began with what I thought was an excellent teaching strategy that quickly and unexpectedly turned into a huge downer. Then, just as quickly and unexpectedly, it turned into a huge upper—one of the most positive and impactful strategies of my career. As is often said, sometimes it's better to be lucky than good.

## A Little Background—
## Teaching High School Social Studies

Among the high school subjects I taught were U.S. History, American Government, and World Studies. You might have vivid memories of how off-the-wall excited you were to take courses like those back in your own high school days.

My daily challenge was, DON'T BE BORING! I tried to make all three courses interesting and enjoyable for thirty-plus teenagers five days a week. (As Ziglar said, speaking is a lot easier than teaching.)

My students were pretty leery when I told them that current events were part of each course. So I charmed them into believing that the assignment would be not only fun and interesting but also *easy* (another teenage favorite). Best of all, it would make them worldly. Actually, it *was* pretty easy: find five headlines per day that cover important events other than sports and entertainment and be able to explain them in two sentences.

We spent the first five to ten minutes of each class reviewing the day's news and newsmakers. My students did, in fact, become well informed in a short time. Some of them even admitted that it was kind of cool, and not really nerdy, to know about things that were going on in the world besides the most recent celebrity scandal. Those who did their short homework were, in fact, beginning to feel more mature and sophisticated. And I was one happy teacher.

## Then Came the Downer

After about four or five days of flaunting their new-found knowledge of world affairs, my students had a realization. Darnell, an insightful and funny kid, expressed it best by smiling and saying, "You know, Mr. Urban, for being such a positive guy, you sure give a negative homework assignment." My brilliant response was something like "Huh?" I went on to point out and glorify the positives of the assignment: they were becoming well informed while doing wonders for their grades. But Darnell came right back with, "Yeah, but reading the news is such a downer. It's all *bad* news. Isn't there anything good going on in the world?" That changed everything.

I assured Darnell and his classmates that plenty of good was happening in the world, but unfortunately, it rarely showed up in the news. That tidbit of information evoked an immediate and logical question: "Why not?" I explained that the news media discovered many years ago that bad news sells, good news doesn't. "If it bleeds, it leads." (More about this in the next chapter.) At the same time, I was still digesting Darnell's comment about me being a positive guy, yet starting class every day with something negative. I was committed to the current events plan, but darn it, I had an image to uphold. I said, "I'll think of something," while praying silently that I actually would.

### Then Came the Upper

My mind was drawing blanks, but I *had* to try something, even if it was dumb. It wouldn't be the first time. So, the next morning I started class with my dumb question: "Who has good news?" It turned out to be not so dumb after all. Unsurprisingly, my students responded with puzzled looks until someone asked, "What do you mean?" followed with "Can you give us some examples?" Seemingly out of nowhere, this question popped up in my mind: "What's something good that's happened in your life or in your family in the past few days?"

They *loved* that question! The floodgates of positivity opened. I'll never forget the first student contribution to our good news time. Sandy shared a personal and touching story about some recent healing in her family. "We're all so happy," she said, "and it feels so good to share this." Her classmates responded with applause, "Yay!," "So cool," "Awesome," and even a tear or two. Sandy took my caring community concept to another level. Something happened that day, and the atmosphere in class, already good, brightened and warmed considerably.

Sandy's expression of some genuine joy was an encouragement for others to share things that brought happiness into their lives. The kids got right to it, and within a few seconds we were hearing all kinds of positive and joyful news. A lot of happy faces, cheers, and laughter were present as the energy level went up in this 8:00 a.m. Government class. We were on to something.

My classroom had a lot of positive signs on the walls. Now I needed a new one and I wanted to have it at the front of the room the next morning. After the last class that day, our art teacher made a great sign for me.

## WHO HAS GOOD NEWS?

The next morning, I put the sign near the top of the chalkboard, about two inches above my head when I stood under it. After the first bell rang, I went to my usual spot just outside the doorway and individually welcomed each student as they came into the room. That was one of the most fun and energizing things I did as a teacher. I got about 150 warm greetings daily, including big smiles, hugs, laughter, and high-fives. How many people get that kind of love on the job every day?

After the students were in and the last bell rang, I quickly took attendance and then went over to stand under my new sign. The kids had already commented on it: "Cool sign, Mr. Urban. Now let's hear about all the good stuff that's going on!" And off we went, sharing our good news. Their involvement grew as they found and shared more and more good news, and the process livened and warmed up the classroom atmosphere. The kids felt more connected and came to know each other a lot better.

## Paying More Attention

It's hard to put into words how profoundly these five minutes of sharing good news every day affected all of us. I had to limit the sharing to five minutes, or it would have gone on for the entire period. The most frequent comment heard went something like this: "I guess I just never paid much attention to all the positive things going on around me. We seem to take all the good in our lives for granted instead of appreciating it like we should." I couldn't have said it better myself.

At the beginning of this chapter are two quotes from Shannon, a former student. The first was a note she left me just a few days before graduating from high school. She said she would take our good news time with her and she was a woman of her word. We've stayed in touch for many years, and she, like so many others, found ways to brighten the lives of others as well as herself by making good news time part of both her personal and professional lives. She wrote the second note and sent it by email when she retired thirty-seven years later.

> Who doesn't love good news?
> Sharing good news means
> sharing happiness.
>
> —T. D. Jakes
> Bishop, author

## Would This Work with Adults?

During the same years I taught in a public high school south of San Francisco, I was also an adjunct professor at my alma mater, the University of San Francisco. (Second jobs are helpful for teachers who want to feed their families.) Teaching adults at USF at night was almost as joyful as teaching kids during the day. I had the best of both worlds.

At the university I taught a series of courses in Organizational Behavior. The program was designed for working adults who, for one reason or another, never went to college right out of high school, and now saw the merit in earning a degree. Most of them were in their thirties, forties, and fifties, and they were a delight to teach. They gave credence to Mark Twain's claim that education is wasted on the young. I learned a lot myself about other careers and about life in the world of for-profit enterprise.

I taught them in the evening, after all of us had already put in a full day's work. I usually started class with a question: "How's your day been so far?" Some of the responses I heard regularly had to do with

- The high level of stress in the workplace
- The many things that went wrong
- The lack of warmth, joy, and humor at work

I couldn't help wondering if what I did at the beginning of each of my high school classes would create some new energy in a room full of stressed-out adults. I thought it was worth a try. If it didn't work as well as it did with my high school students, there would be no big loss. I told my adult students how I started my classes during the day and then asked, "Do you want to give it a shot, or do you think it sounds like a kid thing?" Much to my delight and surprise, I was greeted with huge smiles all around. Jamal, a friendly and high-energy guy, said with great enthusiasm, "We probably need this more than your high school kids do, especially if anyone had the kind of day I did. Let's go for it!" Everyone else was smiling and nodding.

These adults in demanding, full-time jobs (many in Silicon Valley high-tech positions) needed and appreciated this basic refocusing activity more than my younger students did. It's impossible to explain how dramatically it changed the atmosphere. They left the stress of their jobs behind while they shared the good in their lives with each other. One of the most obvious outcomes was that they got to know each other better, expressed their feelings, and formed stronger bonds of friendship. In their evaluations of the course and the teacher at the end of each semester, this simple sharing exercise always received the most praise—even more than my brilliant teaching.

Many of these adult students were in managerial positions, and several of them started using some variation of "Who has good news?" at work. I still receive feedback about how this exercise has also been implemented in families, places of worship, service organizations, government groups, and a variety of other gatherings. Would this work with adults? The answer was a profound YES!

### Spreading the Word

My life changed significantly after the publication of *Life's Greatest Lessons*. I was surprised and overjoyed to receive speaking invitations, first in the United States and then in-

ternationally. I've been speaking at schools and other organizations since 1995, mostly about good character, positive words, and good news. I'm delighted that so many
people have bought in, spread the word, and provided
feedback. These kind people rave about what good news
time has done for them, their friends, family members,
and colleagues.

This book had been on my mind for a long time, but
the "good news doesn't sell" mantra was still in my head.
Then Josephine, a sweet mother and teacher who had
heard me speak in the Philippines, wrote this in an email:
"Hey Good News Guy, I'm having so much fun doing
'good news' in my family, my church, and in my classroom! My husband even does it at work. Thank you so
much for sharing this simple and powerful way to help
people see the good and lift their spirits. Now, please get
over your belief that good news doesn't sell and get working on that book. People need it more than ever." Thank
you, Josephine.

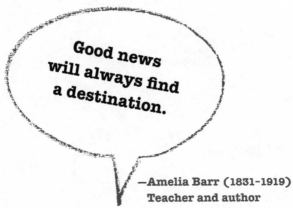

Good news
will always find
a destination.

—Amelia Barr (1831-1919)
Teacher and author

## Good News in Families

I want to end this chapter with a simple suggestion for families. Each evening that you sit down for dinner together, take turns answering this question.

*What was the highlight of your day?*
Just think for a minute about what might happen.
I urge you to try it. Trust me, you're in for a treat.

Whether it's with your partner, your best friend, or your family member, sharing your good news with others can bring all kinds of benefits even beyond the news itself.

—Mona Moieni
**Psychology in Action website**

*People* magazine isn't going to sell very many copies with a headline like this: "Lindsay Lohan enjoys quiet evening reading Robert Frost poems."

—Dave Blanchard
**Senior Editor,** *Industry Week*

## CHAPTER 3

# Bad News Overload

## Negative input can sour your mood

### Becoming Informed

I paid little attention to the main news stories while growing up. I could give you the latest statistics on Willie Mays's batting average, home runs, and RBIs. I could tell you that Elvis's "Don't Be Cruel" was #1 on the pop music charts. But that was about it. I avoided politics because my dad repeatedly and loudly proclaimed that all politicians were greedy and crooked s.o.b.'s (but he didn't say the initials).

My ignorance regarding world affairs changed in college. In my first history class, Dr. Donald Campbell said that we study history so we can have a better understanding of both our roots and the present. He also made an important point about democratic forms of government: they work best when citizens are well informed. Then he paused, smiled, and said, "This is one of the reasons you're in college." He was convincing, and I started paying much more attention to the other news.

> An educated, enlightened, and informed population is one of the surest ways of promoting the health of democracy.
>
> —**Nelson Mandela (1918-2013)**

### Now the Bad News

I considered writing about our need for, and the benefits of, good news for many years. But I kept hearing that good news doesn't sell. The tipping point came on my seventy-ninth birthday. I was healthy, thankful, and happy. Then I began catching up on the latest news. It was so bad that day that it made me wonder if someone should at least *try* to increase our awareness of the good in the world that doesn't get any publicity. Here is a partial list of the news items that triggered the writing of this book.

> News has long centered on negative things because it engages our fear reflex and hence is generally more attention-grabbing.
>
> —**Dr. Tom Stafford Psychology professor, Sheffield, UK**

*In a single day*

- *Time* magazine arrived. The cover story was about hatred in America.

- *The Week* magazine arrived. The cover story was about racial prejudice in America.

- I opened the *San Francisco Chronicle* to the main news section. There were twenty-six articles. Two of them were informational. The other twenty-four all contained bad news. I don't want to pour it on, so below are just half of the headlines I read that day. Nothing will surprise you.

> Wildfire Devastates Town
> E-Cigarettes Hooking Young People
> Massacre Elicits Rage
> Officer Shot and Killed
> Teen Killed in Attack on 12
> Money Controls the Ballot
> Deadly Mosquito Virus Continues to Spread
> Toxic Smog Blankets Festive Event
> Fresh Water Supply at Risk
> Desperate, Hungry Residents Killing
>     Horses to Eat
> Plane Crash Kills 189
> Bribery Charges Against Government Official
> Suicide Bombers Kill 48

My guess is that reading these headlines from the three news sources was not pleasant for you. That's my point. Bad news has a way of bringing us down, and it just keeps coming.

I'm not suggesting that we ignore bad news, nor should we diminish its significance. The pain and suffering it tells of are real, and we should do whatever we can to alleviate at least some of it. Most of us have the opportunity to help in some way, particularly in combating discrimination and supporting the poor. Empathy and kindness always help with healing. Yet our other challenge is to not let the bad news overwhelm us—to offer help where and when we can, but also to learn to balance our negative input by increasing our awareness of what's good and right.

At the same time, we need to understand the two reasons that bad news dominates. One has to do with psychology—how the human brain works. The other has to do with economics—what brings in the money. Hopefully, I can summarize the research of others in a simple and understandable way.

## The Psychological Reasons for Bad News

### 1. We're hard-wired for survival.

Long before we came along, our ancient ancestors were trying to figure out how to live as humans. Number one among their concerns was how to survive, because there were bigger, stronger, faster, meaner, and hungrier creatures out there looking for a meal. This is the simplest way to explain what some psychologists call the fear reflex, the survival instinct, or the

> Negative news has a stronger impact on our minds than positive news. This "brain bias" impacts our daily emotions.
>
> —Hara Estroff Marano
> *Psychology Today*

startle response. Whichever term you prefer, they all mean the same thing, and it explains that we're wired, first and foremost, to defend ourselves and to survive.

Think for a minute about those earliest humans. Getting bad news was absolutely essential to remaining alive. Even before newsprint, radio, phones, and TV, bad news traveled fast. And if you didn't receive it, you were in big trouble. For example, you're walking in the forest looking for some tasty fruit. You hear an ominous sound, the loud footsteps of one of those hungry creatures described above. It's bad news that the hungry beast is crashing your party, but it's good that you have a survival instinct and can hear. The bad news you received, learning that this threatening animal was nearby, just saved your life.

How about your own lifetime? Think about some of the earliest and most important lessons you learned in your childhood. Two of the first words that were drilled into your brain were "NO" and "DON'T." Why? To keep you safe. You probably remember being told to NOT do a lot of things: talk to strangers, walk into the street, put rocks in your mouth, touch the stove, play with matches —the list goes on. The simple reason is that someone who cared about you was teaching you how to survive.

We're wired to defend ourselves, and that gets reinforced as we grow older. Danger gets our attention, and the news media get any threat of it to us more quickly than ever. That can be a good thing if it saves us from harm or death. Yes, the news media often blows things out of proportion, but reporting potential danger is one of their primary obligations. It's something we need and rely upon.

There are a lot of wholesome stories out there waiting to be covered. Then why on earth are we constantly being bombarded with this negativity? There's a reason for it. We secretly love bad news.

—Mayukh Saha
TruthTheory.com

### 2. We have a built-in negativity bias.

A specific part of our brains actually helps us detect danger and inadvertently leads to our negativity bias. Each of us has this tiny, almond-sized watchdog called the amygdala, a built-in early warning system close to the brain stem. Its primary job is to warn us of impending peril. It also provides us with the extra energy we need to get out of harm's way. Those are the good things about the amygdala. The downside is that it often leads us to be overly suspicious and to think negatively. Our job is to use this tiny part of the brain to keep us safe, and then learn to not be overtaken by the negativity.

What psychologists and neuropsychologists call the brain negativity bias is actually an extension of our survival instinct. In modern times we don't have to be on guard every minute of the day as our ancestors did, but we still need to be aware of possible threats. This need can lead to more negativity than necessary and can adversely affect relationships. How? Do you like being around negative people? I didn't think so.

John Cacioppo, PhD, was a psychology professor and researcher at the University of Chicago and one of the leading authorities on brain negativity bias. He assists those of us who aren't science nerds to understand how the amygdala helps protect us. His research and testing showed that our brains react with a greater surge in electrical activity whenever the stimuli are negative. Positive stimuli don't excite the brain as much.

Rick Hanson, PhD, is a leading neuropsychologist at the University of California, Berkeley. His research helps us understand how and why some people develop a bad attitude from consuming too much bad news. He explains that the amygdala uses about two-thirds of its cells to identify negativity. That's its job. But it also *stores* that negativity into our long-term memories, which can lead to excessive negativity. Now we know why some people are so grumpy.

> **Pessimists spread negativity like the flu, and you must limit exposure.**
>
> —Daniel Milstein
> Success.com

## The Economic Reason for Bad News

Plain and simple, we live in a capitalist society. If we own a business that has a hot-selling product, we prosper. If our business has a product that doesn't sell, we crash. The media is a business. It succeeds only when it attracts viewers, readers, and advertisers. The media learned long ago that negative worldviews, angry and violent people, and gory images are big sellers. Sensationalism and fear stir up the amygdala.

Good news may tug at our heartstrings, but it doesn't sell. Leaders in the mainstream news media have been urged for years to present a more balanced picture of the world. Their response? They tack on a 30-second clip of a Girl Scout helping an elderly person cross the street at the end of a 30-minute newscast.

## Three-point summary

1. Bad news grabs our attention. Good news doesn't.

2. Bad news helps us survive. Good news doesn't.

3. Bad news sells. Good news doesn't.

### The Negative Effects of Bad News

The American Psychological Association conducted an extensive survey in 2018 about people in the United States who follow the news regularly. More than 20 percent

> This constant churn of harrowing news is physically and psychologically unhealthy, and you don't need to be directly involved in a tragedy to feel its effects. To any concerned viewer, this pain can feel unavoidable or even necessary.
>
> —A. J. Willingham
> CNN Digital

of the respondents said they constantly monitor their social media feeds. This exposes them to the latest news headlines, whether they had intended it or not. Ten percent said they check the news at least once per hour.

> Too much bad news can make you sick.
>
> —Alexandra Pattillo
> CNN health reporter

The major conclusion from the study was that, for many people, news consumption has a downside. More than half the people surveyed admitted to feeling anxiety, fatigue, and loss of sleep. Markham Heid, who writes for *Time*, observed, "Of course, many people feel it's important to stay informed. And it's understandable that news you find concerning could produce stress anxiety. But recent changes to the way everyone gets their news may not be good for mental and even physical health."

Dr. Graham Davey, a professor emeritus at Sussex University in the UK, supports Heid's point by explaining that the problem is getting worse because the news now reaches us faster and with more graphic detail, especially the gory stuff. Davey calls it increasingly visual and shocking, adding that "These changes have often been detrimental to general mental health."

## A Short List of the Major Effects of Bad News Overload

*Bad news can pull your mood downward.*

Dr. Davey's research also shows that negative news changes one's mood from pleasant to unpleasant or from unpleasant to downright nasty. The most consequential result, he writes, is that "Negative news can significantly change an individual's mood—especially if there is a tendency in the news broadcasts to emphasize suffering and the emotional components of the story."

Dr. Davey also explains that if negative news affects mood, it can affect how one perceives and interacts with the world and other people.

*Bad news can negatively affect both
your mental and physical health.*
According to the 2018 survey mentioned above, a majority of people in the United States who follow the news on a regular basis report feeling a wide variety of emotional bummers. Stress-related hormones, specifically cortisol, have been linked to inflammation associated with cardiovascular disease, rheumatoid arthritis, and a number of other serious health concerns. These effects vary greatly from person to person. Some people balance the bad with the good. Some don't.

*Bad news can increase your worries
and make you feel unsafe.*
A friend who knew I was writing about good news recently asked me, "*Is* there any good news? I go to bed wondering whether I'll die from being nuked by North Korea, murdered by someone breaking into my home, or dying in the latest weather catastrophe. The world's never been this unsafe, you know." I've heard several similar comments while writing this. The psychologists who conduct research on the effects of too much bad news conclude that it's not unusual.

*Bad news of a political nature*
*can raise your level of frustration.*

Political news seems to get people the most fired up. The year 2020 ranks as one of the most divisive and volatile periods most of us can remember. Peaceful dialogue often turns into screaming, peaceful protests often turn into violence and property destruction, and each side becomes more entrenched in its beliefs. On and on it goes. No wonder we're often advised not to argue about politics or religion. Politics seems to bring out the worst in us. I found the following on a website called One Line Fun: "Politics is the art of looking for trouble, finding it, misdiagnosing it, and then misapplying the wrong remedies."

These are only a few of the negative effects of too much bad news. But they're enough to make the point.

I'm so glad to conclude this chapter. If I've put you in a bad mood, I'm sorry. The good news is that it will improve in the next chapter.

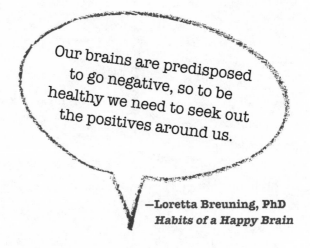

Our brains are predisposed to go negative, so to be healthy we need to seek out the positives around us.

—Loretta Breuning, PhD
*Habits of a Happy Brain*

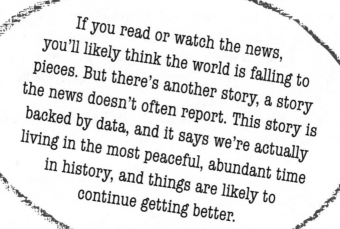

If you read or watch the news, you'll likely think the world is falling to pieces. But there's another story, a story the news doesn't often report. This story is backed by data, and it says we're actually living in the most peaceful, abundant time in history, and things are likely to continue getting better.

—Sveta McShane
SingularityHub.com

CHAPTER 4

# The Good News

*The world is better than the media report*

### Our Worldview May Need Adjusting

One of the books I discovered while writing this one is *Factfulness*, by Hans Rosling. It's fascinating and upbeat, and catalogues facts and extensive research about our current world in an easy and uplifting read. There really is hope for us now and in the future.

Dr. Rosling was one of those amazing people who earned both an MD and a PhD. He used his accumulated knowledge and boundless energy to help people with open minds see the world from a perspective different from that of the news media. Among his many roles, he was a physician, a professor of international health, and a cofounder of the Gapminder Foundation. His mission was to combat ignorance about the present with a fact-based worldview. He also gave some of the most popular TED Talks ever, with more than 35 million views.

Sadly, Dr. Rosling died of pancreatic cancer at age sixty-nine, while at the peak of his contributions. He devoted the last year of his life to completing his book with the help of his son Ola and daughter-in-law Anna. He left behind a great treasure in *Factfulness* and a wonderful legacy of searching for truth to help us better understand our world.

> When we have a fact-based worldview, we can see that the world is not as bad as it seems—and we can see what we have to do to keep making it better.
>
> —Dr. Hans Rosling
> (1948-2017)

## Some Facts: The United States and the World

As I read *Factfulness*, my curiosity about the current state of both the world and the United States significantly increased. I discovered several reliable websites that back up Dr. Rosling's findings. They're worth checking out. Any or all of them will give you a boost.

Being mindful that political nastiness, war, crime, hatred, disease, prejudice, greed, corruption, natural disasters, and other negatives have been and always will be with us, let's take a brief look at some of the marvelous and inspiring trends that are occurring daily, but are rarely mentioned in the news.

Please understand that, for the most part, I'm using my own lifespan to show the progress being made. To refresh your memory, I was born in 1940 and wrote this book in 2020, the year I turned eighty. I hope while reading this, regardless of age, you will also look at the progress made in numerous areas during your own lifetime. I just happen to go back farther than most of you do.

**Education.** Naturally, a teacher looks at this trend first. In the year I was born the high school graduation rate in the United States was 51 percent. By the time I had graduated in 1958 the rate had gone up to almost 65 percent. Today it stands at nearly 84 percent and continues to rise.

In 1940 3.8 percent of U.S. women and 5.5 percent of men had earned college degrees. By the time I earned my bachelor's degree in 1962 the rate had gone up to 6.7 percent women and 11.4 percent men. Today those college graduation rates are almost 35 percent women and 34 percent men. We continue to grow as an educated society. And as the level of our education improves, so does our standard of living.

Literacy and education are also rapidly advancing worldwide. Dr. Rosling places particular emphasis on the increasing educational opportunities for girls, who for centuries were traditionally kept out of schools due to cultural norms and beliefs.

**Health and life expectancy.** In 1940 the average life expectancy in the United States was sixty-two. Today it's a shade under eighty. This is the result of phenomenal advances in medicine and health care, along with an increase in knowledge about the value of a healthy diet and regular exercise. More and more people are living longer and healthier lives.

You may be wondering, as I did, where the United States ranks among countries in the world in longevity. Considering our incredible advances in medicine, shouldn't we be at or near the top? The bad news is that we're not in the Top 30. The good news is that we're #31. Japan tops the list. Others in the top ten are Singapore, Italy, Spain, Switzerland, Australia, Iceland, Israel, South Korea, and Sweden. Why aren't we higher? See above—healthy diet and regular exercise. Many people in the United States still choose neither.

**The eradication of polio.** With all of our recent advances in the treatment of cancer and heart disease, you may wonder why I want to focus on a disease that barely exists in the world today. It's just to put things in perspective from my own life experiences. If you had asked me when I was growing up in the 1940s and '50s what my greatest fear was, the answer would have been polio. It is a brutal and crippling disease that mostly went after young people. Some of my childhood friends were severely paralyzed by it, and I worried about catching it literally every day. It's impossible for anyone born after 1964 to relate to this.

One of the happiest days of my life occurred in my junior year in high school, when I received the Salk polio vaccine. I mention this because countless dedicated medical researchers are currently working on cures for other devastating and fatal diseases, and many more such breakthroughs will happen in the years ahead.

**Democracy and freedom are on the rise.** We read and hear daily about atrocities in the world that are the result of corrupt and dictatorial governments. What we don't read and hear about is the steady growth of democracy and human rights.

According to the Pew Research Center, in 1946 only 29 percent of the world's countries had a form of democratic government. That number had gone down to 24 percent by 1976. But over the next forty years, it grew to 58 percent. With the growth of democracy have come advances in education, health care, an increase in freedom and individual rights, improved economies, a higher standard of living, and happier people.

**Poverty is in decline.** In 2013 my wife Cathy and I took a three-week trip to India. Many of our friends commented, "Why would you ever want to go there? Isn't it mostly poverty?" The answer was, "No, there's much more to it than that," but we didn't convince anyone.

India *is* much more than poverty, and we enjoyed a fascinating experience. India, along with China, are the best two examples of countries reducing the rate of poverty. As recently as 1997, approximately 42 percent of the people in both countries were living in extreme poverty. Today, that figure is 12 percent in India and 1 percent in China, and the numbers continue to go down.

In the United States, the poverty rate was 22 percent when I graduated from high school in 1958. In 2010 it was down to 15 percent and, after some fluctuation, it fell to nearly 12 percent in 2018. The teacher in me believes that as long as we continue to expand educational opportunities throughout the world, we'll be able to bring the poverty numbers even lower.

**Technology is rapidly improving countless facets of life.** Via email, I recently asked one hundred people who grew up in the 1940s, '50s, or '60s what the best development of their lifetime was. More than ninety answered technology. While I asked for a one-word answer, many gave me additional feedback. One of my college friends said, "It's sometimes hard to believe how much better we have it these days. Our cars, phones, tools, TVs, appliances, e-books, cameras, music, lighting, email, websites, videos, clocks, and just about everything else in our homes these days are better." Yes, technology has greatly improved our lives.

If you were born in the 1980s or later, you might have a difficult time understanding what it was like when we older folk were growing up. Amazingly, a lot of us got through college without Google or Wikipedia. We tend to take most of our technology for granted today, so let me go down memory lane regarding two devices we use most days.

- **Telephone.** My parents grew up without one. When I was growing up, we would lift the handset off the cradle and ask the operator to connect us to another number. Later, we went modern and dialed our own numbers without any help. Then came push-button and cordless phones, and then the cell phone. I was about forty-five when I got my first flip phone. It took a few more years before I became really cool and got an iPhone.

- **Television.** Having a TV in one's home didn't become common until the 1950s. We didn't have one in our home until 1955 (my first year in high school). The screen had an odd shape, the picture was in black and white, the reception was fuzzy, and we had just one channel. When I was a junior it doubled to two chan-nels. Color and hi-definition TV were light-years away. I'm still amazed at what we're able to watch on that large, flat, colorful, crystal-clear screen today. And I love all the choices. The telephone and TV are only two examples. Technology continues to make our lives better in literally thousands of other ways.

**Quality of life.** Largely because of advances in education, health care, economics, democracy, and technology, we have the potential to live longer and happier lives. With-out overwhelming you with statistics, here's a short list of some of the other ways in which life is getting better. But you won't read or hear about them in the news. Bad news travels fast, but good news takes the scenic route. The key is to appreciate these advances rather than take them for granted.

- Child labor is dramatically down throughout the world.

- Income is rising in most countries.

- Murders in the United States are in steady decline.

- Travel by car or plane is safer than ever.

- The rights of women, minorities, and LGBTQ+ persons have steadily risen. (Yes, more progress is needed.)

- Access to food and clean water increases daily.

- School bullying is being significantly reduced.

- Home ownership in the United States is near peak level.

- Smoking and other uses of tobacco go down each year.

- There are far fewer teen pregnancies.

- Sports and entertainment get better every year.

- There is more opportunity than ever to have a good quality of life.

The headlines have never been worse. But an increasingly influential group of thinkers insists that humankind has never had it so good—and only our pessimism is holding us back.

—Oliver Burkeman
*The Guardian*

These are but a small percentage of the ways in which the world is getting better. There are countless more. But as Dr. Rosling reminded us, our instincts for fear and negativity, combined with news media that focus on the worst, lead us to believe otherwise.

### Another Look at the Good Old Days

Throughout history adults have complained about the values, work ethic, and behavior of the younger generation while constantly glorifying the good old days. I've never bought into it. As a teacher, I saw great promise in most of my students and reminded them often that they were our future and that each generation has the responsibility of making life better. Life *is* better today because of those younger generations. And the generations yet to come will do the same.

> Believe it or not, the world of the past was much worse.
>
> —Steven Pinker, PhD
> Harvard psychology
> professor

My generation waxes most poetic about the 1950s: post-war economic boom, rock 'n' roll, Elvis, drive-in theaters, soda fountains, the baby boom, the first satellite, the first organ transplant, the expansion of TV, Walt Disney and Mickey Mouse, and on it goes. Ah, those Happy Days.

They were happiest for white males growing up in middle- and upper-class families, but not so hot for a lot of other people. My learning and teaching of history greatly broadened my perspective. Here are a few of the sad realities of that time (all of which I'd been unaware):

- Racial discrimination was widespread and legal.

- During the Korean War almost 37,000 Americans died.

- Smoking increased dramatically.

- Gay, lesbian, and transgender people had to live double lives while hiding their real identities.

- Poverty was far worse than today.

- Women were held back in just about every category except getting pregnant, raising children, and housework.

- Crime increased dramatically.

- There wasn't even a Super Bowl.

> Every generation imagines itself to be more intelligent than the one that went before it, and wiser than the one that comes after it.
>
> —**George Orwell**
> **(1903–1950)**
> ***Nineteen Eighty-Four***

We could compile a similar list of the major negatives in any decade, along with a list of the positives. The point is that the good old days were only better because we tend to have selective memories and a "my generation was the best" mentality. But the truth is that life is better than ever.

## A Few Recommendations

Our progress rarely makes the headlines. I'm deeply indebted to the people who have researched and written about it, and I hope I've condensed some of their main findings into a brief and readable chapter. It could have been five or six times as long.

Let me leave you with two recommendations if you're interested in learning more about how things are actually getting better:

1. Read Dr. Rosling's book *Factfulness*. It's enjoyable to read and will brighten your outlook.

2. Make good use of one of the greatest innovations in history: the Internet. Do a search on "the world is getting better." You won't have time to read all the fascinating articles that come up.

# A Closing Thought

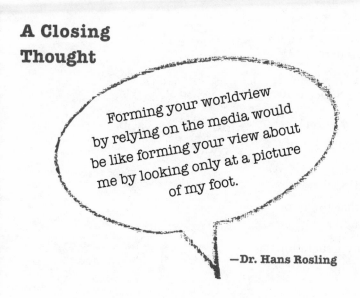

Forming your worldview by relying on the media would be like forming your view about me by looking only at a picture of my foot.

—Dr. Hans Rosling

Just as reading bad news stirs up hormones and sparks neurotransmitters that change mood, so does good news. We can benefit greatly in our personal lives and relationships from exposing ourselves to positive information.

—Celia Abernethy
Thrive Global

If bad news equals junk food, then good news equals fresh fruits and vegetables.

—Justin Osborne
Teacher and blogger

CHAPTER 5

# Happy Hormone Research

*Good news bolsters
health and well-being*

### Reducing Stress and Anxiety

Fortunately, there's been as much research on the effects of good news as there has been on the effects of bad news. While reading studies conducted at ten major universities, I compiled a list of twelve major benefits from the intake of good news. The benefit reported on most frequently and extensively was the reduction of stress and anxiety.

Many of the researchers point out that good news can significantly lessen stress and anxiety while also contributing to peace of mind and a greater sense of well-being. These studies provide scientific evidence that good news and enjoyable experiences make us feel healthier and more optimistic. The more positive information we take in, the better we feel. Obviously, everything can't be positive, but savoring what *is* positive enhances our lives.

Jessica Harrell, PhD, a psychology professor at Western Michigan University, conducted an extensive study on TV news viewing in 2000. She and her colleagues already knew that viewing bad news regularly causes "elevations in anxiety and a generally negative effect." The aim of the research project was to discover if viewing good news leads to the opposite—the lowering of anxiety and a generally positive effect. It did, indeed. The students who took part in that study frequently asked questions afterward that could be crystallized by this one: "If watching and hearing good news is so health-inducing, why isn't there more of it?" There weren't many sources of good news in 2000. There are now, and they grow daily. That's one of the most encouraging discoveries I made while doing my own research.

## Other Benefits of Receiving Good News

Several other benefits come with the intake of uplifting information. I want to list them here without using a lot of the complex scientific terms that challenged me while

The better your brain is at using its energy to focus on the positives, the greater your chances at success.

—Shawn Achor
Founder, GoodThinkInc.com

studying this. I learned about research methods, parts of the brain, and hormones. But I doubt that things like co-variates, the cingulate gyrus, or the names of more than 200 hormones will get you excited. I must admit, though, that the happy hormones (serotonin, dopamine, endorphins, oxytocin), the ones that kick in when we receive good news, are kind of fun. Here are eleven other benefits I found, minus the scientific terms. I'm sure there are others as well.

1. Improves mood

2. Contributes to better mental health

3. Promotes better physical health

4. Leads to a more positive outlook and worldview

5. Raises level of energy

6. Leads to more productivity personally and on the job

7. Increases feelings of gratitude

8. Improves relationships, especially when shared

9. Develops hopefulness about the future

10. Diminishes selfishness while expanding altruism

11. Increases happiness

Obviously, this doesn't mean that, after watching a three-minute clip of news about a little girl being reunited with her missing kitty, your life will suddenly be transformed into an eternal state of bliss. But it *does* mean that positive news has positive effects. The researchers in these studies remind us that bad news gets our attention much more quickly. It's our job, then, to balance it with some positive input.

Another important point: None of the researchers who conducted these studies advises us to ignore all the bad news. That would not only be unwise but almost impossible. A suggestion from a Harvard study was to retrain the brain to absorb more of the positive information available to help us stay balanced.

> While I don't recommend burying our heads in sand and ignoring what is going on around us, we should certainly limit our consumption of bad news and expose ourselves to uplifting content. Consuming good news usually makes us happier and more optimistic about the world, because it reminds us that the world is a good place.
>
> —Tal Ben-Shahar, PhD

These studies also identified five practical suggestions:

1. Decrease consumption of major media bad news.
2. Reduce time spent around negative people.

3. Increase awareness of the many forms of good news.

4. Understand the positive impact good news has.

5. Form the habit of getting a daily dose of positive input.

## Different Strokes for Different Folks

What makes one person feel good doesn't necessarily have the same warm and fuzzy impact on others. The little girl reuniting with her kitty may bring tears of joy to one person while eliciting "What's the big deal?" from another. The reasons for this are simple: our genetic makeups are different, our life experiences have been different, and our brains function differently. We're not all wired the same way. We'd be a pretty boring lot if we were. There's a plentiful supply and a wide variety of good news sources out there. The key is to find the ones that stir up *your* happy hormones. There are several suggestions at the end of this book.

## Good News Comes from a Variety of Sources

Our culture basically has two different understandings of the word *news*. The first refers to the news media—reports about what's currently happening in the world, in our country, and locally. When someone asks us to turn on the news, we understand clearly what they mean. But there's another kind of *news* that also gets our attention. It's information that touches us in a more personal way. This news usually comes from family, friends, colleagues, organizations, and social groups we're part of. Since most of what the media gives us is bad news, we're going to get the bulk of our good news from these other sources. Good news usually comes from life going on all around us. Both my teenage and adult students taught me this regularly.

While they were opening their eyes and ears more to the good around them, they helped me to do the same. One of the most frequent Aha! realizations they shared was expressed by Carlos, who was then thirty-one: "Since the negatives get our attention more naturally than the positives, we'd be better off giving equal time to the positives."

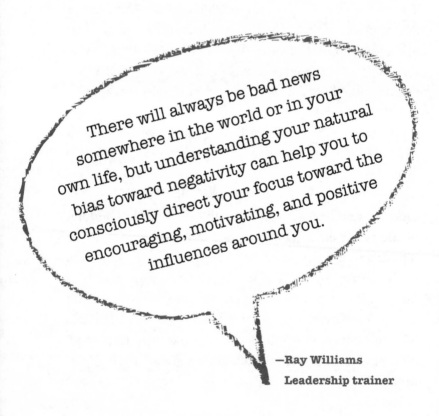

There will always be bad news somewhere in the world or in your own life, but understanding your natural bias toward negativity can help you to consciously direct your focus toward the encouraging, motivating, and positive influences around you.

—Ray Williams
Leadership trainer

I think most of my students, regardless of age, came to this realization. We were retraining our brains even before they started teaching it at Harvard.

## Big News and Little News

When I started asking my adult students who had good news, most of them thought I was referring to what we came to call big news, that is, major life events. So, they were sharing things like a cancer healing, engagements and weddings, big promotions, scholarships, the birth of a child or grandchild, a service award, graduations, a favorite team winning the Super Bowl, a first home, and other occasions of great joy.

I asked, "How about the little news—those not-so-dramatic things that also lift our spirits?" Examples include a call from a friend, help from someone, a new book, tickets to a big game or concert, discovering a new restaurant, a neighbor's chocolate chip cookies, a family event, a compliment, and other little happy events that occur regularly.

Whether major or minor, there's plenty of good news out there. Finding it and spreading it enriches our lives and helps us to realize what Emma Seppala meant when she wrote in *Scientific American*:

Positive experiences happen to us every day, yet we don't always take full advantage of them. Research suggests that we actually have three more times positive experiences than negative. It also shows that discussing positive experiences leads to heightened well-being, increased overall life satisfaction, and even more energy.

> Positive experiences happen to us every day, yet we don't always take full advantage of them. Research suggests that we actually have three more times positive experiences than negative. It also shows that discussing positive experiences leads to heightened well-being, increased overall life satisfaction, and even more energy.
>
> —Emma Seppala, PhD
> *Scientific American*

## A New Version of an Old Sign

I made a follow-up to my "Who has good news?" sign. It was about the same size, but with larger letters.

# GIGO

Naturally, on the day I put it up, my students asked about what it meant. As if surprised, I smiled and answered, "I'm so glad you asked. Let me give you a little history lesson first."

Since high school kids can't imagine life without computers, I told them about the early days, when the term

GIGO was used frequently. It means "Garbage In—Garbage Out," and refers to programming. Flawed or nonsense input (garbage) produces flawed and nonsense output (garbage). The term isn't used as much today, but it still has the same meaning. I said, "Your minds operate the same way. But since you already know that, let's give GIGO a new definition that fits better with what we do."

I suggested Good In—Good Out. If our brains are the personal processors of our lives, and we're free to choose what goes into them (most of the time), it makes sense to put good in. I asked them to give me a few examples, and they had several: uplifting music, happy or funny TV shows, inspiring books, being with fun people, family gatherings, and positive things on the Internet, especially funny video clips on YouTube.

If you want to be happy, then steadily and continuously keep filling your head with what's good in your life. Fill it to overflowing.

—Mike Sullivan
Thought-Management.com

### The Mind Is Like a Garden

"Your mind is like a garden / Your thoughts are the seeds / You can grow flowers / Or you can grow weeds." At least three people have been given credit for this little poem. To whoever said it first, I thank you. It's both clever and wise and makes a good point about caring for the mind. As the poem says, the *seeds* are thoughts, and it takes only a little imagination to realize that the *flowers* are positive words and actions, and the *weeds* are negative words and actions.

As clever as the poem is, it leaves out two important elements of caring for the mind. First, where do the seeds (thoughts) come from? Are you putting in any old seeds that are available, seeds that someone else forces on you, or seeds that you've carefully selected? Thoughts don't just happen. They're the result of what you allow into your processor.

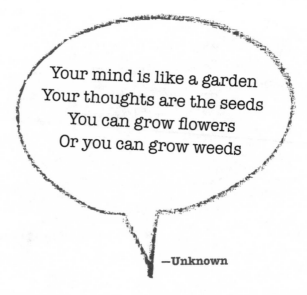

Your mind is like a garden
Your thoughts are the seeds
You can grow flowers
Or you can grow weeds

—Unknown

Second, even if you select the healthiest seeds possible, they need to be nourished regularly. You have to keep the weeds (negative words and actions) out. This requires constant care.

James Allen (1864–1912) was another writer who compared the mind to a garden. His short book, *As A Man Thinketh*, written in 1903, is considered a classic. Popular authors of the past, such as Norman Vincent Peale (*The Power of Positive Thinking*) and Dale Carnegie (*How to Win Friends and Influence People*) were greatly influenced by Allen's book. Many successful business leaders of the twentieth century praise Allen for his work. And modern-day success coach Tony Robbins claims it as his favorite and most influential book.

Allen wrote the book in old-fashioned English (notice that he said *thinketh* rather than *thinks* in the title). I've read this little gem many times over the years, so I'm going to take the liberty to put his overall theme into modern-day English. Here are his main points:

- A person's mind has some similarities with a garden.

- It can be intelligently cultivated or allowed to run wild.

- Whether cultivated or neglected, it will produce results.

- If no useful seeds (positive information) are put into it, weeds (negative information) will take it over.

- You have to put good seeds in, nourish them on a regular basis, and keep the weeds out. It needs good care.

## We Reap What We Sow

Allen's points are yet another way of saying GIGO, whether you're referring to garbage or good. Let's first clarify two more old-fashioned words. *Sow* means plant, or what you put in. *Reap* means harvest, or what you get later. Sow a good lemon seed, care for it, and you'll reap a good crop of lemons from a lemon tree. Many people are familiar with this process because it's in the Bible. Yet actually, the concept of sowing and reaping goes back a lot further. It was considered to be a natural law of the universe, often called karma or the Tao. Ancient teachers like Buddha, Confucius, and others believed that being good puts us in harmony with nature. They taught that goodness leads to individual happiness and a peaceful society.

I do believe reading positive, uplifting, inspiring information every day has made me a better person. Not better than another person, just better than I was before. It's the opposite of my professor's admonition of "Garbage in, Garbage out" philosophy.

—Jennifer Ledet
Ledet Management

What we see
depends mainly on
what we look for.

—John Lubbock (1834–1913)
Banker, scientist, author

We can retrain
the brain to scan for
the good things in life.

—Shawn Achor

CHAPTER 6

# Looking for the Good

*It may require an attitude adjustment*

### Healthy Habits, Healthy Mind

You've probably heard the expression that we're creatures of habit. That was one of the first things I learned in Psychology 1A in college. Neurobiologists and cognitive psychologists tell us that 40–90 percent of our behavior is due to habit, which varies with the individual. Thus many of us are on automatic pilot much of the time. That's not necessarily a bad thing. Habits help us get through our daily responsibilities, and some are actually good habits.

To a large extent, our daily input is the result of habit. We tend to visit the same websites, listen to the same people talk, watch the same TV programs, and read the same printed materials. The amount of that input that is positive or negative varies with the individual. Some of us need to do a little adjusting to find the good.

That's why researcher and author Shawn Achor says we

often need to retrain the brain or, as he often puts it, re-wire it. Habits are easy to form—so easy, in fact, that they often form without our realizing it—and hard to break. Changing habits, particularly bad ones, is a completely different story. One bad habit is allowing too much garbage to be dumped into our minds.

We rewire, or retrain, the brain by getting into the habit of consciously looking for the good, allowing it into our minds, savoring it, and sharing it with others. Can this become a habit? Yes. How long will it take? Psychologists generally agree that if we do something for twenty-one days in a row, we'll form a new habit. One of the best possible habits is a daily routine of positive input.

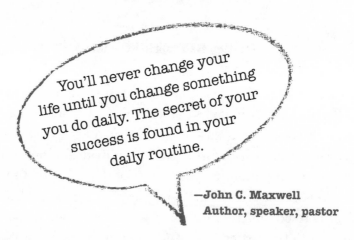

You'll never change your life until you change something you do daily. The secret of your success is found in your daily routine.

—John C. Maxwell
Author, speaker, pastor

## The Psychology of Mental Health and Happiness

Writing a book about what goes into the mind and what comes out in a life without mentioning psychology would be like writing a book about Elvis Presley without mentioning music. Psychology is foundational here. So that we have the same understanding of the word, let's use this definition provided by the American Psychological Association: "Psychology is the scientific study of the mind and behavior." That is concise and clear, as in what goes on in the mind comes out in behavior. Psychology, by its very nature, also studies what goes *into* the mind.

Another course I taught in high school, my favorite, was an introductory course in developmental psychology open to twelfth graders as an elective. At the university I taught a series of courses in organizational behavior, which is basically psychology and sociology applied to the work-place—how people behave in organizations.

Attitude, thinking, mindset, outlook, and many related terms are all integral in the field of psychology, because they lead to feelings and to action that we call behavior. What all of this is leading up to is the field of . . .

### Positive Psychology

Without trying to explain the long and complex history of psychology, I want to cover some of the major trends. Positivepsychology.com does an excellent job of briefly explaining four waves in the field.

1. **Disease model.** Focused on abnormal behavior and mental illness. Sigmund Freud (1856–1939) comes to mind, along with words like neurosis and phobia.

2. **Behaviorism.** Focused on the influence of environ-mental forces and how we're conditioned by them. The big names were John B. Watson, Ivan Pavlov (and his dogs), and B. F. Skinner.

3. **Humanistic psychology.** Focused on our perception of the world around us and the meaning we give to it. It is often referred to as human potential psychology. Two big names in the field were Carl Rogers and Abraham Maslow.

4. **Positive psychology.** Focuses primarily on authentic happiness, meaning, and quality of life. As opposed to studying mental illness, positive psychology studies the factors contributing to mental health. Martin Seligman is generally considered the founder of this field. He taught at the University of Pennsylvania and is currently the director of the Positive Psychology Center. His books *Learned Optimism* and *Authentic Happiness* helped propel the movement.

To give you an idea of the impact this trend in psychology has had, let's go to Harvard University, established in

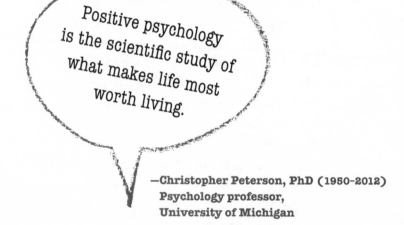

Positive psychology is the scientific study of what makes life most worth living.

—Christopher Peterson, PhD (1950-2012)
Psychology professor,
University of Michigan

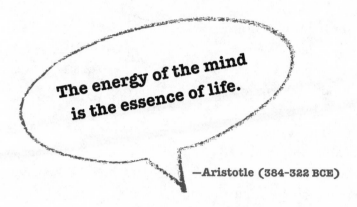

The energy of the mind is the essence of life.

—Aristotle (384–322 BCE)

1636. In 2006, a record 1,400-plus students enrolled in Positive Psychology 1504, a course taught by Dr. Tal Ben-Shahar with the assistance of Shawn Achor. The course consisted of twenty-two lectures of an hour and fifteen minutes by Ben-Shahar and a guest lecture on humor by Achor. It was one of the most popular courses ever taught at Harvard. The primary focus was answering this question: How can we help ourselves and others become happier? The question in no way suggests that anyone can be happy all the time. Pain and suffering do exist. How we deal with it is key. As a friend once told me, "Pain is inevitable; misery is optional." By the way, these days you can watch both Ben-Shahar and Achor on YouTube. Their talks will provide valuable input for your mind without having to pay Harvard tuition, and might even help you rewire and energize critical parts of your mind.

## Life's Control Center

One of the most valuable things I ever learned was taught by a college classmate, Bruce Diaso, who had been severely crippled by polio. He was in a wheelchair and could not move his arms or legs. He could talk and move his head, hands, and fingers —that was it. We lived in nearby dorm rooms and had some classes together, so we saw each other frequently.

> The control center of your life is your attitude.
>
> —Norman Cousins
> (1915-1990)

When I met Bruce, he greeted me warmly, and my first thought was, "Poor guy." I felt genuinely sorry for him and wondered how he was able to do common daily tasks like get out of bed in the morning, go to the bathroom, shower, comb his hair, get dressed, and go to breakfast. I had always taken the ability to do those things for granted.

I learned later that Bruce was one of the last persons in the United States to be afflicted by polio (in 1957). He got through college with the help of seven caretakers. One was his roommate, and the other six lived in rooms nearby. They took care of his every need. I always admired them because they were so caring.

Most notable about Bruce were his smile, warmth, energy, genuine interest in other people, sense of humor, curiosity, number of friends, and overall positivity. The more I was with him, the more amazing he became. Everybody loved Bruce, not because they felt sorry for him, but because he was such a joy to be around. I always wondered how he stayed so positive. So, I asked.

Bruce told me that when he got polio and realized he would never walk or even lift his arms again, he wanted to die. He said self-pity and anger were overtaking him.

But his primary doctor issued a challenge that dramatically changed his life. His doctor said, "I understood why you have those feelings. I would, too, if I were your age and polio brought me down."

Then his doctor asked him, "Are your self-pity and anger making things better for you, or are they making things worse? I think you're poisoning your mind, Bruce, and it's making it harder for me and my colleagues to help you. You have to help us help you. We don't want that great brain of yours to go to waste. You have a life ahead of you, and you have something to contribute. So, let me leave you with six words that I want you to think about: "Change your attitude, change your life." The doctor smiled and said, "Please think about it, Bruce. I'll talk to you tomorrow."

Bruce *did* think about those six words. "In fact," he told me, "I couldn't get them out of my mind. I *was* poisoning myself and was also preventing myself from moving on with life. I realized that I needed to replace the poison with thoughts and words that were more health-inducing. So, I read extensively about psychology and how best to deal with adversity. Instead of poisoning my mind, I wanted to nourish it. After only a day or so, it was actually pretty easy to dump my self-pity and anger and replace them with two words that are far more nourishing." By this time while listening to him, I was ready to jump out of my chair. Excitedly, I asked him, "What are these two magic words? Please share these secrets of life!" He smiled and calmly said, "Hal, there's no magic involved and there are no secrets—just two simple words that I've trained my-self to live by. They changed my attitude, and they *did* change my life. Those two simple words are *thankfulness* and *opportunity*."

Please keep in mind that at the time I was a not-so-worldly eighteen-year-old college kid who was often clueless. And that was one of those times. I wondered what Bruce could possibly be *thankful* for, and what he meant by *opportunity*. So, I asked.

**Thankfulness.** Bruce said he had learned to change his focus from what he *didn't* have and *couldn't* control to what he *did* have and what he *could* control. He had loving parents and family members, great friends, his mind, a good education, faith, freedom, a bright future, and the ability to learn, help others, and contribute to the greater good. He listed several other things that I had always taken for granted. And I wasn't paralyzed.

**Opportunity.** Bruce said he had trained himself to say the same thing every morning when he woke up: "Thank you, Lord, for this day. Help me to see all the opportunities that come with it." He said he actually had fun throughout the day looking for opportunities to feed his mind with positive and inspiring information. "It helps me keep the poison out," he affirmed with a big smile.

> You are what
> you feed your mind.
>
> —Reverend Ike
> (1935-2009)

Bruce graduated from college with highest honors, and then from law school with highest honors, and became a successful attorney. He received many honors for his free legal work for charitable organizations and public service. All of this success came because he learned that his attitude was the control center of his life and that it was his choice in both good and bad times.

> The greatest discovery of my generation is that human beings can alter their lives by altering their attitudes of mind.
>
> —William James
> (1842–1910)

## Viktor Frankl's Legacy

About ten years later a friend gave me one of the most influential books I have ever read: *Man's Search for Meaning*, by Viktor Frankl. Frankl was a Holocaust survivor. When he was a young and accomplished professional, everything that mattered to him was taken away: parents, wife, other family members, friends, home, all his possessions, his medical practice, and his freedom. But after all this loss and indescribable suffering, he wasn't quite ready to give up. Frankl decided that if he could figure out something the Nazis could *never* take away, he would defeat them. And he *did* defeat them, because he found it.

> Everything can be taken from a man but one thing: the last of the human freedoms—to choose one's attitude in any given set of circumstances, to choose one's own way.

—**Viktor Frankl (1905-1997)**

Frankl never denied the suffering and horrors of the Holocaust. He wrote in detail about many of the unthinkable atrocities of the prison camps. Still, he wanted to pass on what he learned: that we *can* survive pain and suffering and loss. We're still free to choose how to deal with them. My friend Bruce is a good example. We all go through hard times. But we'll always be free to feed our minds with information that heals and helps us find the good.

### The Main Point

Telling stories about a young man with polio and a Holocaust victim may seem inconsistent with the main theme of this book, the benefits of taking in positive information. But what Bruce Diaso and Viktor Frankl and many others have taught us *is* incredibly positive. Millions of people have absolutely no awareness that attitude is their control center, and even less awareness that they have a choice of attitude. They put their lives on autopilot, not paying attention to what goes into their minds, and instead follow popular culture, as in follow-the-follower.

One of my favorite leisure-time activities is reading, mostly books about personal growth and good character, positive psychology, and biographies. I read about people who have contributed mightily to our progress, who have overcome great odds, who have inspired us, and who have passed on valuable life lessons. One thing the people described in these books have in common is that they always looked for positive and nourishing information, including reading books and seeking advice from wise people. This kind of input helped them develop attitudes that led to achievement. They proved over and over that having the right attitude is at the center of our lives. Maybe that knowledge is why Keith Harrell (1956–2010) titled his 2000 book *Attitude Is Everything*.

People who choose generally positive attitudes expect the best; people who choose negative attitudes expect the worst. In both cases, those expectations are usually fulfilled. Positive people accept that attitude is a choice. Negative people don't; they always find someone or something to blame.

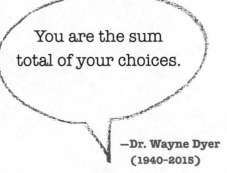

You are the sum
total of your choices.

**—Dr. Wayne Dyer**
**(1940–2015)**

## Four Things I Wanted My Students to Remember

1. You have a free will—the freedom to make choices.

2. You choose your attitude—the control center of life.

3. You choose what goes into your mind—good or bad.

4. What goes into your mind comes out in your life.

Just an attitude adjustment. It made my whole outlook brand new.

—Hank Williams, Jr.
Country singer

Cultivate the habit of being grateful for every good thing that comes to you, and to give thanks continuously. And because all things have contributed to your advancement, you should include all things in your gratitude.

—Ralph Waldo Emerson
(1803–1882)

The happiest people in the world aren't the ones who have the most. The happiest people are the ones who are the most thankful for what they have.

—Ruth Urban
(1913–2009)

# Count Your Blessings

*Thankful people find the most good*

When I was about ten and having one of those woe-is-me days, I was moping around complaining that some kids in our neighborhood were sporting some really cool jeans called Levi's. I, on the other hand, was wearing cheaper and dorky-looking jeans made by another company. How shameful. I complained about having to wear uncool jeans only when my dad wasn't around. He'd have cuffed me upside the head and told me how hard he worked to buy those jeans, and that I should be happy to have clothes.

My mom, quite a bit gentler, smiled and softly told me some family history. She told me about growing up on a farm in Missouri, how difficult life was, and how little they had. The pictures she showed me made the point even more strongly. She said I not only had more *things*, but a more comfortable life, and more opportunity. Then she said, "The happiest people in the world aren't the ones who have the most. The happiest people are the ones who are the most thankful for what they have." Those words stuck with me.

My mom seemed to be ahead of her time in understanding how gratitude plays a major role in well-being and happiness. Her common sense has been borne out by important findings from extensive research that has since been done on gratitude.

When you're thankful, you tune in more to the goodness around you. We quickly and naturally notice the negatives of life. But with a little rewiring and a little diligence, we can train ourselves to see that the positives far outnumber the negatives. Once this becomes a habit, the good around us seems to increase. You won't even have to look for it. It will start finding you.

> Gratitude helps you to grow and expand; gratitude brings joy and laughter into your life and into the lives of those around you.

—Eileen Caddy (1917-2006)
Teacher, author

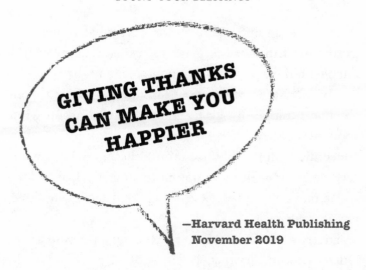

**GIVING THANKS CAN MAKE YOU HAPPIER**

—Harvard Health Publishing
November 2019

## What Research Tells Us about the Effects of Gratitude

"Giving Thanks Can Make You Happier"—This is actually a headline rather than a quote. Among the many resources for mental health and happiness I recently discovered is Harvard Health Publishing, a consumer health division of Harvard Medical School. I particularly like its motto: "Trusted advice for a healthier life." It regularly publishes articles on its website dealing with a variety of health matters. The relationship between thankfulness and happiness is found in the category called Mind and Mood.

Here's a quote that summarizes the article cited above: "In positive psychology research, gratitude is strongly and consistently associated with greater happiness. Gratitude helps people feel more positive emotions, relish good experiences, improve their health, deal with adversity, and build strong relationships." That seems like a pretty good argument for developing and maintaining thankfulness.

In one such study, participants were divided into three groups. Each group was given a writing assignment over the next ten weeks. One group wrote about their daily irritations; another wrote about how events affected them, whether positive or negative; and the third group wrote about what they were grateful for during each week of the study. It's probably no surprise that those who wrote about gratitude felt more optimistic in general, and better about their own lives. Several reported feeling healthier physically as well.

Dr. Robert Emmons, a psychology professor at the University of California, Davis, is often described as the world's leading scientific expert on the psychology of gratitude. He has also written a number of books on the subject, including *The Little Book of Gratitude: Create a Life of Happiness and Wellbeing by Giving Thanks*. Dr. Michael McCullough, a psychology professor at the University of Miami, has collaborated with Emmons and has also researched and written about how gratitude and forgiveness contribute to happiness.

Dr. Martin Seligman of the University of Pennsylvania has also conducted research on thankfulness. In one of his studies, he asked more than 400 people to write and hand deliver a letter of appreciation to someone who had influenced them in a positive way, but whom they had never thanked properly. He was surprised that of all the strategies he employed, this one had the strongest and longest-lasting positive effects. The people who wrote the letters reported a huge surge in their happiness scores. This particular expression of thankfulness results in the ultimate win-win scenario. The person receiving the letter is both surprised and deeply touched, and the person delivering it increases in happiness by bringing such joy to someone deserving it.

One unexpected, but not surprising, result of these many studies on gratitude is that the people who participate in the studies and then see the results report later that they have an increased awareness of the good around them. It isn't so much that they now *look* harder for the good; they simply *notice* it more. It has been there all along.

> The thankful heart opens our eyes to the multitude of blessings that continually surround us.
>
> —James E. Faust (1920-2007)
> Church of Latter-Day Saints leader

I own several excellent books about thankfulness and gratitude and have enjoyed reading each. What surprised me most in these books was the extent of the research conducted in recent years, which highlights two points: first, the many benefits of being thankful, and second, the recommendations for increasing thankfulness and well-being in yourself. Here are a few of those recommendations.

- Send a hand-written note of thanks to someone who has enhanced your life.

- Keep a gratitude journal for at least twenty-one days. At the end of each day, jot down the events, things, and people you're thankful for.

- Pray and/or meditate. Depending on your beliefs, try either of these by sitting quietly with your eyes closed and focus on the people, activities, and things that add joy to your life. The more you do this, the more effective it becomes.

- Put a short quote or message about gratitude on your nightstand. Read it just before you turn off the lights. Read it again when you wake up in the morning.

- Look for the good around you throughout an average day. Try to notice the things you normally take for granted.

- Take a walk through your residence, be it a home, apartment, or other. Look at everything in each room. Are you thankful you have these things?

- Carry a pocket reminder.

I have two examples of this last recommendation. A Jewish friend of mine carries a small coin in his pocket at all times. On one side it has the Star of David; on the other side are the words *Modeh Ani*, which means "I give thanks."

A woman at one of my speaking engagements shared her story about rocks with me—not Pet Rocks, but Thank Rocks. She keeps a smooth rock about the size of a baseball on her desk. It has the word *THANK* painted on it. She keeps a smaller one in her purse. She said with a big smile, "We all need reminders to help us pay attention to the good in our lives."

In case you're wondering, you can buy religious and non-religious coins or stones with a message of thankfulness on them, and you can order custom engraved stones online.

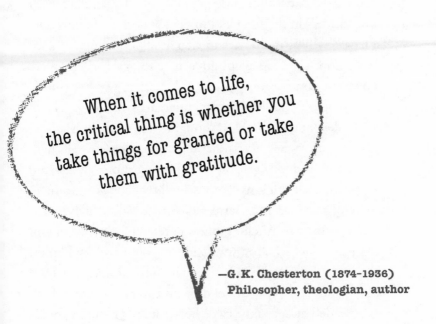

When it comes to life, the critical thing is whether you take things for granted or take them with gratitude.

—G. K. Chesterton (1874-1936)
Philosopher, theologian, author

> **The most fortunate are those who have a wonderful capacity to appreciate again and again, freshly and naively, the basic goods of life, with awe, pleasure, wonder, and even ecstasy.**

—Abraham Maslow, PhD
(1908-1970)

### A Routine Day Experiment in Noticing the Good

In my early days of teaching psychology, I began to wonder what leaders in the field had to say about thankfulness. Did it have anything to do with mental health or happiness? This was before the field of positive psychology had emerged. The most positive form of psychology then was humanistic psychology, also called human potential psychology. One of the leaders of this school of thought was Abraham Maslow, whose primary belief was that the average person sells her/himself short and is capable of achieving more success and happiness in life. He is famous for his theory of the hierarchy of needs and the term *self-actualization*, which means coming closer to reaching one's potential for a meaningful and joyful life. Maslow was, and still is, one of my heroes. His research and writing had a huge impact on my teaching and on my life. Near the end of his career and life, which sadly ended at age sixty-two, he wrote, "The most fortunate are those who have a wonderful capacity to appreciate again and again, freshly and naively, the basic goods of life, with awe, pleasure, wonder, and even ecstasy."

Wanting to share this capacity to appreciate what Maslow wrote about, I asked my high school and adult students how many times in a routine day they stopped to think about these basic goods of life. This led to a wonderful, eye-opening discussion about what those goods are.

> When you notice something, you automatically become more present to it. You encounter it more fully. And it requires very little effort on your part to do this.
>
> —Jane E. Dutton, PhD
> Professor Emerita,
> University of Michigan

My instructions were: As you go through your day, from getting up in the morning to going to bed that evening, write down one or more things you're thankful for relating to each activity. I asked them to bring their lists to the next class. To put it mildly, the ensuing discussions were among the happiest and most meaningful in my teaching career. Both the kids and adults were equally amazed at how many good things they usually overlook in an average day. I can sum them up in three comments:

1. "We sure take a lot of the good things all around us every day for granted."

2. "We should stop and think once in a while about how good we have it."

3. "We complain about so many of these things. We should be giving thanks for them."

### Can You Go One Day without Complaining?

Another meaningful assignment related to our thankful-ness exercise was the Bruce Diaso Challenge: Go 24 Hours without Complaining. I named it after Bruce because, in all the years I knew him, no one ever heard him complain about anything. After telling both my high school and adult students Bruce's story, I issued the challenge.

It led to a lively discussion about whether anyone could do it or not. The first high school student who spoke up said, "I don't think I could go five minutes without com-plaining." Then we heard, "I don't know; not complain-ing for a whole day would *really* be hard." Another one said, "Not hard, impossible." We all laughed. I asked them if they wanted to give it a try, and most did.

I've been issuing the Bruce Diaso Challenge for more than fifty years. It took me twenty-three years to find someone who could do it. Her name is Grace. Since then I've found about six more people who succeeded. Most people give up in the first hour.

> If you don't like something,
> change it. If you can't change it,
> change your attitude.
> Don't complain.

—Maya Angelou (1928-2014)
Author, poet, civil rights leader

> **Be grateful for what you have and stop complaining. It bores everybody else, does you no good, and doesn't solve any problems.**
>
> —Zig Ziglar

Does this make the assignment a failure? No—it was a huge success. Here's what both the kids and the adults have said about it:

- "I didn't realize how much I complain."

- "I guess complaining is really a habit—a bad one."

- "I think we're *conditioned* to complain."

- "We live in a culture of complaint."

- "It seems like *everybody* complains way too much."

And my favorite: "I told my dad that our homework assignment was to go twenty-four hours without complaining. He asked, 'What the hell kind of assignment is that? I thought they were supposed to teach you something of value in school.'" Just a reminder that you can't win 'em all.

### The Opposite of Complaining Is Expressing Thanks

Let's wrap this up by returning to thankfulness, especially expressing it. Not long after the Bruce Diaso Challenge came another of my favorite assignments. I gave each of my students a paper with four columns on it. Each column had twenty blanks underneath. Here's what the headings mean.

**I'm thankful for . . .**

| Things (1) | Things (2) | People | Other |
| --- | --- | --- | --- |
| _____ | _____ | _____ | _____ |
| _____ | _____ | _____ | _____ |
| _____ | _____ | _____ | _____ |

**Things (1).** Any material object that you or your family owns that you're thankful for. I urged students to mentally walk through their homes, look at everything they have, and ask themselves: "Would I want to be without this?" Small things take on new meaning.

**Things (2).** These are also material objects, but don't belong to you or your family. You have access to them because they're part of your community and are intended for the common good. Examples: paved roads, stores of all types, groceries, parks, schools, places of worship, banks, and so on.

**People.** Any person in your life who has had a positive influence on you. It must be someone you know, or have known, personally. They could be alive or no longer with us. This column isn't about celebrities you don't know.

> There are plenty of ways
> to be happier and more productive
> instead of complaining.

> —Ciara Conlon
> *Chaos to Control*

**Other.** This one may stump you for a while, but once you get the hang of it, it will increase your appreciation for your free choices. *Other* means an intangible—that is, what you have but can't touch. Examples are freedom, love, kindness, learning, and opportunity.

I urge you to give this exercise a try. Not all in one sitting—just do it when you feel the need for a lift. I have former students, some now in their sixties, who tell me they've filled several sheets (eighty blanks on each), and keep adding as they go along. Stories like that warm a teacher's heart.

I've done this exercise with people of all ages and in many walks of life all over the United States and in several other countries. After almost every presentation people stay to share a personal story about learning to be more thankful. A teacher in Cartagena, Colombia, wrote this quote on the back of her business card and gave it to me several years ago:

> **The roots of all goodness
> lie in the soil of appreciation
> for goodness.**

> —The Dalai Lama

Whether it's one good friend
or a dozen, healthy social
connections promote physical
well-being, longevity, and
optimal mental health.

—Suzanne Degges-White, PhD
Counselor, Northern
Illinois University

## CHAPTER 8

# Good Friends, Good News

*They help us live healthier and longer*

### When Friends Become Good News

I'm aware that not everyone associates friendship with good news. I've been linking the two for more than fifty years and hope that after reading this chapter you'll do the same. Back when my students and I started sharing good news at the beginning of class, one day, in response to our *Who has good news?* opening question, Gary smiled and raised his hand. He said, "The best news I have is that my new friends at this school are getting me through some tough times. They're good news every day."

Gary grew up in Southern California and had started his senior year there. His dad got a job offer he couldn't refuse, had to start soon, and the family was quickly off to the San Francisco Bay Area. It was a real trauma for Gary to move to a new town 400 miles away, a new neighborhood, and a new school, all in a matter of weeks. He was in shock and on stress overload by the time he got to our school. But there's some good news here.

I had some incredibly kind and caring kids in that first-period class. They had bought into my Golden Rule/Win-Win caring community philosophy and bonded with each other quickly. I learned about Gary's situation the day before he showed up and was able to tell my students they were getting a new classmate. I told them he was having to move and change schools in his senior year and asked them to make him feel welcome and help him fit in.

Those kids not only rose to the occasion but also went well beyond it. They did everything possible to help Gary feel like he belonged, not only in class, but in school and in the social life surrounding it. We watched Gary blossom. I had a lot of wonderful classes in my career, but these kids will always hold a special place in my heart.

When Gary made the comment linking his new friends with good news, he also told his classmates how much he appreciated them. He teared up while doing it. I think everyone else in the class, including me, teared up as well. It was one of those touching moments a teacher never forgets.

Gary's words that day also led to a meaningful discussion about how good friends really *are* good news. It wasn't uncommon for the kids to affectionately greet each other with "Hello, Good News," instead of a name, for the rest of that school year. And I never grew tired of them calling me "Good News Guy."

Gary thrived in his new school with the help of his new friends. They brought out the best in him. He did well and

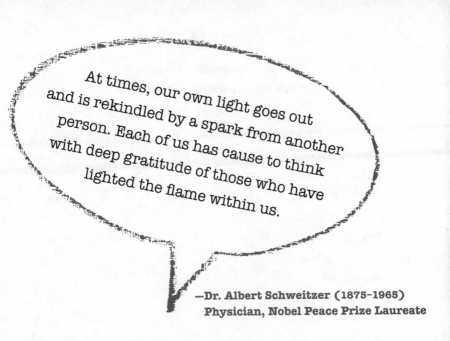

At times, our own light goes out and is rekindled by a spark from another person. Each of us has cause to think with deep gratitude of those who have lighted the flame within us.

—Dr. Albert Schweitzer (1875-1965)
Physician, Nobel Peace Prize Laureate

went on to college and a successful career. Don't you just love happy endings? It all started with good friends who were also good news.

### A Brief Reminder before Moving On

In the introductory pages of this book I supplied definitions of key terms used throughout. So you don't have to thumb back, here are two definitions we're using:

- **Good News.** Anything you see, hear, or read that makes you feel good. This includes seeing people you like (even pictures of them or seeing their names) and anything that makes you laugh.

- **Input.** Information going into your mind, whether put there by someone else or chosen by you.

## What Research Says about
## Friendship and Quality of Life

The Mayo Clinic and Harvard Medical School are two of the many trusted institutions that have conducted research on the effects of friendship on our health and happiness. In fact, I was both surprised and delighted to find so many studies done in this area. Emily Sohn wrote in the *Washington Post* in 2016: "Ever since researchers began to make links between loneliness and poor health about 25 years ago, ago, the scientific literature on the value of friendship has exploded. Today, the data make a convincing case: Having people who care about us is good for us." The results I present here are from a variety of studies conducted

Friendships enrich your life and improve your health.

—**Mayo Clinic Staff**
**MayoClinic.org**

Good connections and social support can improve health and increase longevity.

—**Harvard Health Publishing**
**Harvard.edu**

not only by Mayo and Harvard, but by National Public Radio, *Psychology Today*, and the Ohio State University College of Medicine.

The seven benefits of friendship listed below are essentially abbreviated. I could write two or three pages on each while explaining the types of research conducted. But that would make this chapter too long and tedious. I do encourage you, if you'd like more details, to put your search engine to use on the benefits of friendship.

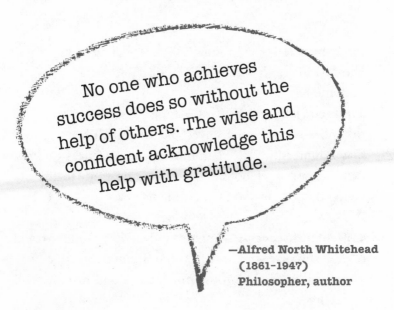

No one who achieves success does so without the help of others. The wise and confident acknowledge this help with gratitude.

—Alfred North Whitehead
(1861-1947)
Philosopher, author

### Seven Things Good Friends Do for Us

**1. Physical health** is significantly better among people with strong social networks. Those who socialize often feel better and live longer than people who are lonely.

**2. Mental health.** People who spend time with friends reg-

> Friendship improves happiness, and abates misery, by doubling our joys, and dividing our grief.

—Cicero (106-43 BCE)
Roman philosopher

ularly have fewer emotional issues. A feeling of belonging helps us feel both secure and comfortable.

**3. Fun and laughter.** The more time we spend with friends, the more we enjoy ourselves and laugh. It's been proven that laughter boosts our immune systems, burns calories, and increases metabolism. There's some truth to the old saying that laughter is the best medicine.

**4. Mental sharpness.** Being around people we enjoy and respect stimulates brain cells. New insights and discoveries shared by friends arouse our interest and make us feel more alive.

**5. Good advice.** Good friends often act as mentors, helping us make better decisions. They also urge us to step outside our comfort zones and try new ventures.

**6. Empathy and comfort.** We often turn to friends during hard times because they understand us and are in a position to extend comfort and support. Good friends have a calming effect during times of pain and anxiety. They also help us show more concern for others.

**7. Increased joy.** Time spent with friends stirs up the happy hormones in our brains. Life is simply a lot more fun and interesting when shared with friends.

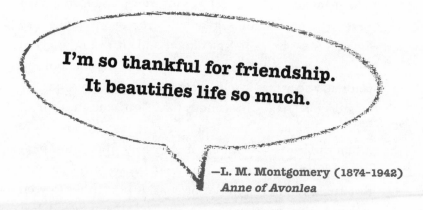

**I'm so thankful for friendship. It beautifies life so much.**

—L. M. Montgomery (1874-1942)
*Anne of Avonlea*

### Friendship Is an Investment That Pays Rich Dividends

We're fortunate that many bright scholars are deeply committed to helping others lead more productive and happier lives. One of them is Shawn Achor, whose book *The Happiness Advantage* I've used extensively. A few of my beliefs regarding friendship and mental well-being have been verified by Shawn's extensive research and his own writing. In *The Happiness Advantage*,

**Social support is your single greatest asset.**

— Shawn Achor
*The Happiness Advantage*

he explains seven principles that lead to a quality life. The seventh is called Social Investment. I loved the concept of *investing* in our relationships. Thank you, Shawn.

Many of us who grew up in earlier generations were exposed to classic pieces of literature in school. One such piece was "Self-Reliance," an 1841 essay written by philosopher and author Ralph Waldo Emerson (1803–1882). The main advice Emerson had for us was to be your own person, think for yourself, avoid being overly influenced by others or by popular culture, and that "nothing can bring you peace but yourself." I read it in high school and still remember that it sounded pretty cool and macho.

Achor refers to this famous essay as practically a rite of passage, but he believes strongly that it's the other way around. We succeed the most with help from other people. He says one of the biggest mistakes we make early in our careers and even in our personal lives is to try to go it alone. An overwhelming body of research conducted during the past thirty years tells us just the opposite. That's why Achor claims that social support is your single greatest asset.

Achor actually goes back much further than the research of recent years. He points out that evolutionary psychologists established many years ago that we are all born with a natural need to affiliate with others for a variety of reasons. That need has been literally wired into our biology. He explains what happens to us physically and emotionally when we form strong social bonds: "When we make a positive social connection, the pleasure-inducing hormone oxytocin is released into our bloodstream, immediately reducing anxiety and improving concentration and focus. Each social connection also bolsters our cardiovascular, neuroendocrine, and immune systems, so that the more connections we make over time, the better we function." In other words, it's not some psychological or philosophical theory that tells us to socialize. It's our bodies. We have a biological need for healthy social relationships, not only to survive but also to grow and prosper.

What happens to people without a strong social network? They become ill physically and psychologically, as a result of loneliness. Dr. John Cacioppo, a University of Chicago psychologist, studied loneliness for more than thirty years and then wrote the book *Loneliness: Human Nature and the Need for Social Connection* in 2008. His major conclusion was that loneliness can be as deadly as some diseases. He cites one national survey of 24,000 workers that found that both men and women with few social ties were far more likely to suffer from major depression.

Another study on loneliness is actually one of the longest-running psychological studies ever conducted. It's called the Harvard Study of Adult Development, or Harvard Men Study, and is still ongoing. It has been following 268 men who entered Harvard in the late 1930s and has stayed with them through the present. Yes, a seventy-year research project. For the last forty years it's been conducted by psychologist George Vaillant. He has analyzed the data in great detail

> Surround yourself only with people who are going to lift you higher.
>
> — Oprah Winfrey

and has come to this conclusion: "Seventy years of evidence that our relationships with other people matter, and matter more than anything else in the world."

Nothing is more precious than friendship.

—Moufid Mansour
Egyptologist

## A Great Reminder at the Luxor Temple

One of the most fascinating trips Cathy and I have taken was to Egypt in 2006. We saw all the famous sites, were fascinated by the culture, and had a guide who might be the most loved person in his country. His name is Moufid Mansour. He seemed to know everything about Egypt and every person in it. Wherever we went, people went out of their way to greet him with huge smiles, shouts of joy, and full-body hugs. They were elated to see him. It added great joy to our daily adventures along the Nile.

One day at the famous Luxor Temple we were having coffee with him. I said, "Moufid, I can't believe how many friends you have. Everyone is so happy to see you." Without hesitating for a second, he smiled broadly and said something I'll never forget: "Nothing is more precious than friendship."

He went on to say that "Seeing good friends is like receiving good news. It always makes us feel better. It energizes us, makes us feel loved, and reminds us to be thankful for how our friends enrich our lives." Later that day Cathy and I talked about how Moufid had helped us develop a greater appreciation for our friends and how much they enhance our lives. That's why it's always good news whenever I see or hear from one of them.

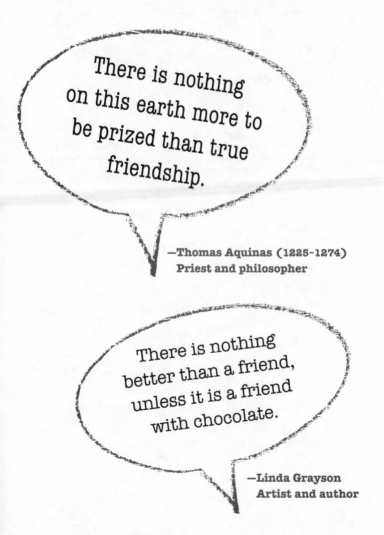

There is nothing on this earth more to be prized than true friendship.

—Thomas Aquinas (1225-1274)
Priest and philosopher

There is nothing better than a friend, unless it is a friend with chocolate.

—Linda Grayson
Artist and author

We have experienced how wonderful it feels to receive praise and gratitude from others. It is equally wonderful to give praise.

—Sir John Templeton (1912-2008)
Founder, Templeton Foundation

When words are both true and kind, they can change our world.

—Buddha (480-400 BCE)
Philosopher, spiritual teacher

## CHAPTER 9

# Pass It On

*Spreading good news is always win-win*

### How This Chapter Is a Little Different

Up to now this book has been about what goes into your mind and who puts it there. This chapter is about what *you* put into other people's minds.

Let's begin with these questions: How often do you put positive and uplifting information into the minds of others? Do other people think "good news" when they see you coming or see your name on an incoming email? Many years ago, a friend taught me a life-changing lesson. He said every day of our lives we have the opportunity to add joy to the lives of those around us.

### On Being a Life-Enhancer

The highest compliment I can give another person is to say that she or he is a life-enhancer. Life-enhancers are people

> My parents taught me something really valuable when I was five and heading off to kindergarten: "If your words might hurt someone, don't say them. If your words can add joy to someone's day, shout them out."

—Tim Hansel (1941-2009)
Teacher, author, speaker

who consistently make life better for the people they have contact with. Sue Wighton, writing in *The Courier Mail* in Australia, defines such people this way: "Life-enhancers add sparkle to the meaning of life." That's too good to leave out. Let's go with both definitions.

For one magical year back in the early 1970s, Tim Hansel and I were members of the same high school faculty, even members of the same department. He had transferred from another school in the district, and within a short time he came to be one of the best and most loved friends of my life.

Our friendship began by having lunch together in his classroom early in the year. We were already tired of the gossip and complaining we heard in the faculty dining room, so lunch with Tim became a daily thing. After a short time, I wanted to know more specifically what made

Tim tick. How did he become such a positive and life-affirming person? How did he become so joyful?

One thing really stood out. I had never heard Tim say anything negative. I told him that was one of the things I liked most about him and asked if there was a story behind it.

Tim broke out in a bigger smile than usual and said, "There sure is!" He felt he started life luckier than most people because both of his parents were intelligent, loving, caring, and funny. They had a family mission statement and explained it as a standard by which they lived each day. A colorful sign hanging in their kitchen said, ALWAYS HAVE SOMETHING GOOD TO SAY. Tim said he tried hard to live up to it, not only to honor his parents but also to reap the rewards. He said it always feels good to make someone else feel good. Tim did it more than anyone I've known. He was a master life-enhancer.

He also showed me a little reminder he carried in his pocket to help him stay focused on his family mission statement. It was a passage from the New Testament,

Do not let any unwholesome talk come out of your mouths, but only what is helpful for building others up according to their needs, that it may benefit those who listen.

—Ephesians 4:29

Ephesians 4:29: "Do not let any unwholesome talk come out of your mouths, but only what is helpful for building others up according to their needs, that it may benefit those who listen."

Tim drew comfort and strength from his faith, but he didn't preach or broadcast it. He respected others' beliefs. He made the point that his little reminder didn't say anything about God or religion. He called it flat-out great advice for anyone, no matter what they believe or don't believe.

The passage from Ephesians is similar to a passage from the Quran carried by one of my former adult students named Yusuf, who is a Muslim: "Speak that which is kindest." I didn't know Yusuf as well as I knew Tim but saw him weekly. He was also a life-enhancer and always had a good word. He shared his pocket reminder when we were

> Speak that which is kindest.
>
> —Quran 17:53

> We are wired by nature to be elevated at the sight of other people's goodness.
>
> —Mark Matousek
> Author, agnostic

learning about Islam in a course on world religions I was teaching. It was Yusuf who reminded us that if we look at the teachings of all faiths, we'll find something about speaking kind and uplifting words to others. Sharon, a staunch nonbeliever in the class, felt a need to remind everyone that we don't have to believe in God or any religious system to spread kindness and joy with our words. Her point was well accepted by her classmates. One of them even said "Amen!"

### What If You're an Introvert?

Can introverts be life-enhancers? My students asked this question every time I talked about life-enhancers. The answer is yes. Many people claim that they're too shy, quiet, or introverted, but you don't have to be wild and crazy and bubbly to be a life-enhancer. My response is always a

> You need to be aware of what others are doing, applaud their efforts, acknowledge their successes, and encourage them in their pursuits. When we all help one another, everybody wins.

—Jim Stovall
*The Ultimate Gift*

story about my mom. She was a humble and gentle person who never wanted to be the center of attention. But she took a genuine interest in others, showed that she cared, and had a kind word for everyone. She wanted to make other people happy. And she did or said whatever made that happen. That's why she was so loved. She was a life-enhancer—a quiet, soft-spoken one.

> I learned that we are all broadcasters, and by changing the stories we transmit, we can create positive change. We do it by broadcasting happiness.
>
> —**Michelle Gielan**
> *Broadcasting Happiness*

## Anyone Can Broadcast Happiness

Michelle Gielan has also conducted extensive research in the field of positive psychology. She worked in the mainstream news media for five years. The bad news eventually wore her down. She's now devoted to doing the opposite: spreading good news and helping others do the same. She urges people in all walks of life to share the positive and believes strongly that anyone can do it.

Michelle suggests we start every kind of communication with something positive. Some of those different types of encounters are talking to a friend in person or on the phone, writing an email or text, starting any type of meeting, conversing with a customer of your business, talking to family members, meeting a person who is new to you, even writing a report. Getting things off to a positive start sets the tone for the conversation in each situation.

Michelle says it all starts with changing our outlook. She calls it refocusing our attention. If we don't see the good around us, it won't be in our minds, and it won't be what we talk about. If we let our natural tendencies rule us, we'll be far more likely to talk about what's wrong instead of what's right. What comes out of our mouths is usually the result of what got our attention and landed in our minds. Look for the good. When you find it, share it with someone.

Happiness is the only thing that multiplies when you share it.

—Dr. Albert Schweitzer (1875-1965)
Physician, Nobel Peace Prize Laureate

## Having More Fun While Greeting Others

Does the following exchange between two people who know each other sound familiar?

**Bill:** Hi, Sue.

**Sue:** Hi, Bill.

**Bill:** How are you?

**Sue:** Fine. How are you?

**Bill:** Fine.

Bill and Sue either go their separate ways or start a conversation, depending on the circumstances. How many times a day does the above exchange, or something similar, occur? I doubt that anyone has researched this, but my guess is that the answer is somewhere in the millions.

I used to hear it about 150 times a day, five days a week. I'm not exaggerating—it was often more than 150 times. Remember, I stood at the door and individually greeted my students before class started. I did this for two reasons: First, I wanted my students to feel welcome. Second, a huge transfusion of energy happened at the door each time the greeting took place. As you know, teenagers have a lot of energy. That's what I liked most about them. And each time I received a warm greeting at the door it revved me up. I told the kids I was like a rechargeable battery. If I got thirty or more positive greetings before class started, I would be fully charged and be a much more energetic and fun teacher that day. They thought I was kidding, but I was actually telling the truth. We do, in fact, transfer energy into each other.

I started doing this back in the late 1960s and, because I did it five times a day, I became increasingly aware of the ritual of "Hi. How are you? Fine." It challenged me to come up with something less routine, more creative, and more fun. It didn't take long. All I had to do was ask myself a simple question: "How do you *really* feel each time a student gives you a warm greeting?" It was a lot more than "fine." I was genuinely happy to see almost all of them, so I needed to tell them. Here was the exchange the next day:

Maria is the first student to show up for my 8 a.m. class. I'm at the door. She smiles at me.

**Me** (*also smiling*): Hi, Maria.

**Maria** (*still smiling*): Hi, Mr. Urban. How are you?

**Me** (*still smiling*): I was good, but I'm a lot better now that I've seen you.

**Maria** (*now with a bigger smile and laughing*): Oh, Mr. Urban, you're so funny.

**Me** (*still smiling*): I'm glad to make you laugh, but I wasn't trying to be funny. Seeing you first thing in the morning really does make me happy.

**Maria** (*still smiling*): Oh, Mr. Urban, you're so sweet.

Now, please think for a moment about what took place in this greeting that lasted about 30 seconds. Maria was glad to see me. I was glad to see her. We made each other feel good. She felt appreciated, even touched. She made me feel as though I was both funny and sweet. How's that for win-win in record time? Please understand that I don't share this story because I want you to think I'm some kind of hero. I'm not. This was another one of those dumb-luck ideas that popped into my head simply because I was a little bored with Hi.-How-are-you?-Fine. I did this with both my teenage and adult students for most of my career. Did I ever get bored with it? Never. Did I ever get tired of saying the same thing so many times in one day? Never, because there are so many variations of "I was good, but I'm a lot better now that I've seen you."

Here are a few examples (all with a smile):

How are you?

"Really good now that you've shown up."

"As good as it gets when I see *you*."

"Better every time I see you."

"Really happy now that you're here."

"I'm so thankful that you're one of my students."

Four or five students come to the door at the same time. One of them asks, "How are you?" I answer, "Way better now that you guys are here." I probably had thirty to forty variations of it. The possibilities are endless. And it was always fun and uplifting for two people, the student I greeted and me.

How about outside of school? Did I, or do I, greet friends like this? I did, and still do greet anyone I know and like with "I was good, but better now that I've seen you," or one of its many variations. The response? Always laughter if it's the first time they've heard it. Maybe the first ten times. Following are some of the other responses I've heard from adult friends over the years. Men and women differ.

**WOMEN**

"Oh, you're so nice (sweet, thoughtful, funny, kind, cute, etc.)."

"Oh, you probably tell all the women that."
My response: "No, just the ones I like."

"Thank you. I'm glad I have that effect on you." (*all with smiles or laughter*)

**MEN**

"Good one." (*while laughing*)

"You're so full of it." (*while laughing*)

"I seem to have that effect on people." (*while laughing*)

"You say that every time I see you."
My response: "It's true every time I see you."

Guys I see every day—for example, at the gym each morning—often come up to me and, before I can greet them, ask, "Are you better now that you've seen me?" My answer: "I sure am. Seeing you this early in the morning is going to make my whole day better." We both laugh.

**EMAIL STARTERS (MEN OR WOMEN)**

"Hi, Chris. It's always good news to see your name pop up."

"Hi, Pat. Good news! I just got an email from a special friend."

"Hi, Sam. It's so good to see your name first thing in the morning."

Your first thoughts in the morning can have a huge impact on the attitude, feelings, and energy you carry around with you for the remainder of the day.

—Elyse Santilli
Life coach, blogger

### Final Suggestion: Get Off to a Good Start

You're far more likely to find good news and pass it on to others if you start your day on a positive note. A simple way to make this happen is to try to begin each day with some positive input. Plenty of research tells us that how we start the day sets the stage for the rest of it. As Mary Poppins said, "Well begun is half done."

I know some of you are thinking, "But I'm not a morning person. It comes way too early." And others are thinking, "I have too much to do each morning. I don't have time to meditate or go outside and smell the roses." I understand. But even if you're not a morning person or are crunched for time, you can still start your day in a positive way. Life coach Elyse Santilli emphasizes that "Your first thoughts in the morning can have a huge impact on the attitude, feelings, and energy you carry around with you for the remainder of the day." The thoughts can come from a variety of sources, and they don't have to take a lot of time.

The key is to put something that makes you feel good in a place where you'll see it first thing in the morning. It could be a picture of a person you love or an occasion you never want to forget. It could be your favorite quote, or a book that's had a lasting impact on you. It could even be a single word or two, such as Bruce Diaso's *thankfulness* and *opportunity*. It could be an object with a positive memory. You've heard that breakfast is the most important meal of the day. So is what you feed your mind first thing in the morning.

When you arise in the morning, think of what a precious privilege it is to be alive—to breathe, to think, to enjoy, to love.

—Marcus Aurelius
(121-180 CE)

## What Your Kind Words Do for Others

> Kind words are short and easy to speak, but their echoes are truly endless.

—Mother Teresa (1910–1997)
Catholic nun, Nobel Peace Prize Laureate

> We increase whatever we praise. The whole creation responds to praise, and is glad.

—Charles Fillmore (1854–1948)
American mystic

# What a Teacher Always Hopes For

During my thirty-six years in the classroom, I always wanted to be upbeat and interesting. I also wanted to teach something that would enrich my students' lives and would stay with them. I have the same goals when I write. A book becomes my classroom.

While I haven't been able to give you a warm and friendly greeting each time you opened this book, I do hope that we made a connection (and that I kept you awake). I also hope you learned something of lasting value.

In closing, I wish you a continual stream of good news, now and in the years to come. And, please, be good news to others. Let me leave you with some final words of wisdom from two women I greatly admire.

> Let no one ever come to you without leaving happier and better.
>
> —**Mother Teresa**

I've learned that people will forget what you said, people will forget what you did, but people will never forget how you made them feel.

—Maya Angelou

# Sources for More Good News

This section was added at the request of friends and colleagues who viewed the original manuscript of this book. They suggested I include information about people, organizations, and current movements devoted to the expansion of good news.

I can't cover all of them for two reasons: there are literally too many, which is a good thing, and many new sources have emerged since this book was completed. I urge readers who want to learn more about recent developments to do a web search on sources of good news. What I'm reporting on are the people and organizations (all with websites) that already have a successful track record.

> Good news comes in many forms.
>
> —Janet Langsam
> CEO, Arts
> Westchester

## Two Promising Trends in News Reporting

While the emphasis here is on people and organizations who provide good news regularly, it's important to at least introduce two movements in journalism that are growing in influence. They're similar, but use different names.

### *Constructive journalism*

World's Best News defines it this way:

> Constructive journalism is a response to increasing tabloidisation, sensationalism and negativity bias of the news media today. It is an approach that aims to provide audiences with a fair, accurate, and contextualised picture of the world, without overemphasising the negative and what is going wrong. While a healthy dose of negativity in the press is undoubtedly necessary, the chronic overexposure of negative [news] constitutes a hidden media bias that has an erosive effect on the societies we live in. . . .
>
> Our constructive journalism is based on:
>
> - a focus on progress, possibilities and solutions to the big challenges facing the world today . . .
>
> - building relations with our readership by inspiring hope and belief that we can change the world

See WorldsBestNews.org for more information.

### *Transformative journalism*

Definition: An activating, engaging, solution-focused approach to covering news. It does not ignore serious issues facing our world; it covers them in depth in a way that activates the belief that our behavior matters, enables social engagement from readers and viewers, and provides actionable solutions to the issues covered.

The website MichelleGielan.com has an entire section on Transformative Journalism. One of the headings states: "The formula for news coverage is broken. Transformative Journalism is the way forward." At the end of her book *Broadcasting Happiness*, Gielan writes: "If you have questions about Transformative Journalism or want to join this movement, I would love to hear from you." She can be reached at transformativejournalism.com.

## Q & A with Leaders in the Field

Another of the great joys in writing this book was to converse with prominent people in both positive psychology and the good news movement. I'm deeply thankful for the knowledge, advice, and time of these kind and brilliant leaders. Here is a brief description of each, along with their answers to my questions.

### Martin Seligman, PhD

Dr. Seligman is regarded as the father of positive psychology. He is a professor at the University of Pennsylvania, a researcher, and the author of several best-selling books. He has also written extensively about virtues, good character, and their relationship to a happy and meaningful life.

**Question:** What are the main benefits of feeding the mind with positive information?

**Dr. Seligman:**
1. Better vagal tone—hence better cardiac health.
2. Better mood, more zest.

3. More hope for the future (optimism).
4. More realism (media are way out of proportion).
5. Less depression, less anger, less anxiety.

Vagal tone: If this term is new to you, as it was to me, a brief explanation may help. The vagus nerve is a fundamental component of the nervous system. The stronger your vagal tone is, the stronger your body is at regulating blood glucose levels, reducing the likelihood of diabetes, stroke, and cardiovascular disease. This means good news is good for the heart.

### Tal Ben-Shahar, PhD

Dr. Ben-Shahar is known as one of the leading teachers and authors in the field of positive psychology. His Psychology 1504 class was one of the most popular ever taught at Harvard. He is currently a serial entrepreneur as the co-founder of Happiness Studies Academy, Potentialife, Maytiv Center, and Happier.TV.

**Question:** Please compare media news and good news.

**Dr. Ben-Shahar:** Media news—The media is not a looking glass but a magnifying glass. It doesn't merely reflect reality but accentuates a particular part of it. The media is a source of much negativity and unhappiness because many of our societal ills, from violence to drugs, from obsession with body image to superficial materialism, are not merely reflected in the media, they are magnified by it.

Good news—being exposed to positive information benefits us emotionally, physically, and mentally. It can contribute in a meaningful way to a happier and healthier life.

## Michelle Gielan

Michelle hosted two national news programs at CBS News in New York. Bad news took its toll. She wanted to remain a news broadcaster, but also wanted to cast more light on the better side of life. Since 2010 she has done research on the news media, written a best-selling book called *Broadcasting Happiness* (2015), founded the Institute for Applied Positive Research, and become an executive producer of The Happiness Advantage on PBS.

**Question:** Now that you've moved from the mainstream media news to a more positive type of broadcasting, what advice do you have for people who want to do their part?

**Gielan:** I learned that we are all broadcasters, and by changing the stories we transmit, we can create positive change. Every word we say during our day counts. And we get from this world what we give. Whatever news we broadcast to one another, in person or online, shifting the balance of news toward the positive and transmitting a solutions-focused, empowered reality pay dividends on many fronts. Our words matter.

## Shawn Achor

Shawn spent twelve years at Harvard conducting research and teaching, some of it with Dr. Ben-Shahar in positive psychology. He is the author of six books, starting with *The Happiness Advantage.* Shawn has spoken in more than fifty countries and gave one of the most popular TED Talks ever. He lectures on PBS.

**Question:** You frequently speak and write about our need

to retrain the brain. How does this apply to the types of information we allow or put into our minds?

**Achor:** We start by grasping the difference between *noise* and *signal*. *Noise* is information that is negative, false, or unnecessary. *Signal* is information that is true and reliable and alerts you to opportunities, possibilities, and resources that will help you. Our brains have to actively decide what to toss out and what to listen to and absorb. We can choose either to hear negative, flawed, or irrelevant information or to absorb information that will help us.

### Geri Weis-Corbley

Geri has more than thirty-five years in television production and online news media. After working in mainstream media, she came to believe we were receiving a distorted picture of both the world and daily events. In 1997 she launched the Good News Network (GNN.org). She calls it an antidote to the barrage of negativity experienced in the mainstream media. She became the first expert in the field of positive news and has been dubbed Good News Guru by the *Washington Post*.

**Question:** What was your primary motivation in founding the Good News Network?

**Weis-Corbley:** I created GNN because the media was failing to report enough of the positive, and it was simply too hard to find good news in quantities large enough to make a difference in one's mental health. Letters I've received over the company's twenty-two-plus years strongly support the notion that positive news helps improve both physical and mental health.

## Organizations Making a Difference

These organizations happen to be the ones I used most frequently while writing this book. Again, they're a starting place. You may find many others to be of value. Most of the descriptions offered below come from their websites. They can describe their mission better than I can.

### *Good News Network*

goodnewsnetwork.org

Not only does this site offer good news on a daily basis, but it also allows you to subscribe for free and receive an email with at least four good news stories each weekday.

Mission: The website, with its archive of 21,000 positive news stories from around the globe, confirms what people already know—that good news itself is not in short supply; the broadcasting of it is. GNN is a daily dose of hope.

### *Greater Good Science Center*

greatergood.berkeley.edu

This isn't so much a daily good news site as it is a resource center for mental health and personal growth based on solid research. The center was founded in 2001 at the University of California, Berkeley. It offers seven different newsletters you can subscribe to. The basic one is Greater Good Magazine, which will be emailed to you twice per week.

Mission: "We study the psychology, sociology, and

neuroscience of well-being and teach skills that foster a thriving, resilient, and compassionate society."

## Huff Post Good News

huffpost.com/goodnews

*The Huffington Post* was founded by Arianna Huffington in 2005. It's now the Huff Post, and in 2012 she added an option: "Huff Post Good News, a section that will shine a much-needed spotlight on what's inspiring, what's positive, what's working, and what's missing from what most of what the media chooses to cover."

The site uses "a variety of storytelling tools to bridge the wide gap that separates the world as it is from the world as portrayed by the bulk of the media."

## Thrive Global

thriveglobal.com

Thrive Global is another Huffington creation. It's not the type of site that reports good news, but it *is* a site devoted to health and well-being, especially for those in the workplace. Good news is good for our health and our mood, but there are other factors involved. Huffington describes what she learned this way: "I became more and more passionate about the connection between well-being and performance. As I went around the world speaking about my experience, I saw two things: First, that we're facing a stress and burnout epidemic. And second, that people deeply want to change the way they work and live."

She launched Thrive Global "to create something real and tangible that would help individuals, companies, and communities improve their well-being and performance."

## Smile Therapy

smiletherapy.com

Smile Therapy offers a wide variety of uplifting messages. It's run by Tim Smith, a man who lives and breathes the subtitle of this book: "Feeding your mind with what's good for your heart." The site's sections include Life Lessons, Inspirational Stories, Humor, Creativity, Thoughtfulness, Gratitude, Common Sense, Music, Encouragement, and Videos.

Smile Therapy offers a Monday–Saturday subscription to a positive message every morning. You can begin with a free 30-day trial. Tim's mission: "In my time I've consumed approximately 180,000 pages of inspiring content from books alone. All of this reading has helped me take a completely different approach to life, one that I really want to share with the world."

## Ever Widening Circles

everwideningcircles.com

"Ever Widening Circles is an online publication on a mission to change the negative dialogue about our times. We celebrate the insights, innovations, and good news that prove it's still an amazing world with the promise of no ads or politics."

The founder, Dr. Lynda Ulrich, is a practicing dentist and an energetic human connector. She says this about EWC: "In 2014 I assembled a team that began curating the web for insights and innovations going uncelebrated. And now, we've published over a thousand articles that point to the work of ingenious problem-solvers, thought leaders, and wonders all around the globe."

There are plenty more out there. I did a web search on "sources of good news" and found more than fifty. I wish you much enjoyment and enrichment while searching for and finding the good.

## Oldies but Goodies

Let's not forget that at least eight sources of good news and happy hormone activity have been around for a long time. I'll close with them as wisely described by experts.

**Books**

All that mankind has done, thought, gained, or been; it is lying as in magic preservation in the pages of books.

—Thomas Carlyle
(1795–1881)
Historian

**People**

Hang out with people who bring out your best.

—Beth Kuhel
Executive Leadership Coach

**Faith**

It doesn't matter where we worship
or what we call God; there is only one,
inter-dependent human family. We are born
for goodness, to love—free of prejudice.

—Archbishop
Desmond Tutu

**Lifelong learning**

The more that you read,
the more things you will know.
The more that you learn,
the more places you'll go.

—Dr. Seuss (1904-1991)

**The Web**

You can learn
anything on the
Internet.

—Ben Bajarin
TIME.com

## Music

It doesn't matter what song you listen to, music has the capability to change your mood from bad to good. Listening to your favorite music triggers the brain to release the feelgood chemical called dopamine that could help fade away a bad mood.

—Saliha Nasline
*The Economic Times*

## Exercise

People who exercise regularly tend to do so because it gives them an enormous sense of well-being. They feel more energetic throughout the day, sleep better at night, have sharper memories, and feel more relaxed and positive about themselves and their lives.

—Lawrence Robinson,
Jeanne Segal, PhD,
Melinda Smith, MA
Helpguide.org

The good news is that moderate-intensity aerobic activity, such as brisk walking, is generally safe for most people.

—Centers for Disease Control and Prevention website

## Helping others

We do ourselves the most good doing something for others.

—Horace Mann (1796–1859)
Father of public education

# References

Achor, Shawn. *The Happiness Advantage*. New York: Penguin Random House, 2010.

————. *Before Happiness*. New York: Penguin Random House, 2013.

Allen, James. *As A Man Thinketh*. New York: St. Martin's Press, 2019 (originally published 1903).

Ben-Shahar, Tal. *Happier*. New York: McGraw-Hill, 2007.

————. *Even Happier*. New York: McGraw-Hill, 2010.

————. *Choose the Life You Want*. New York: The Experiment, 2012.

Cacioppo, John, and William Patrick. *Loneliness: Human Nature and the Need for Social Connection*. New York: W. W. Norton & Company, 2008.

Dalai Lama (Lhamo Thondup) and Archbishop Desmond Tutu. *The Book of Joy*. New York: Penguin Random House, 2016.

Emmons, Robert A. *The Little Book of Gratitude*. New York: Hachette Books, 2016.

Frankl, Viktor. *Man's Search for Meaning*. New York: Washington Square Press, 1963.

Gielan, Michelle. *Broadcasting Happiness*. Dallas: BenBella Books, 2015.

Jackson, Jodie. *You Are What You Read*. London: Unbound, 2018.

Maslow, Abraham. *Toward a Psychology of Being*. New York: John Wiley & Sons, 1999 (originally published 1962).

Rosling, Hans. *Factfulness*. New York: Flatiron Books, 2018.

Seligman, Martin. *Learned Optimism*. New York: Vintage Books, 1991.

———. *Authentic Happiness*. New York: Simon & Schuster, 2002.

Vilhauer, Jennice. "The Mental Wellness Routine That Will Change Your Life." *Psychology Today*, March 28, 2017.

Weis-Corbley, Geri. *. . . And Now, the Good News*. Santa Barbara: Good News Network Publishing, 2018.

Ziglar, Zig. *See You at the Top*. Dallas: Pelican Publishing Company, 1974.

# Acknowledgments

I learned long ago that writing a book and getting it published would be one of the toughest challenges of my life. Nothing has changed. The key is finding the right publisher, the right editor, and the right support team. I'm happy to say that I struck the mother lode on all three.

**Publisher**. The mission of Berrett-Koehler Publishers in Oakland, California, is "Connecting people and ideas to create a world that works for all." I learned during my first visit that these are far more than nice-sounding words. They authentically represent the culture of the company, and I'm honored to now be part of it.

**Editor**. Neal Maillet has been everything an author wants and needs—a constructive critic, an advisor with keen insight and acute language skills, a professional with a cheerful sense of humor, and a good friend. Thank you, Neal, for always being there and for all you've done to make this a better book.

**Support team**. Jeevan Sivasubramaniam and Valerie Caldwell are two leaders on the Berrett-Koehler team who also live up to the company's mission. Jeevan was always there with help on logistics. Valerie was always there with help on design and the cover. Thank you, Jeevan and Valerie.

Carol Metzker, Ellyn Kerr, and Joseph Webb—my three reviewers. Thank you for your professionalism, time, vision, and suggestions. The valuable input from each of you also made this a better book.

# About the Author

Hal Urban earned bachelor's and master's degrees in history, a California teaching credential, and a doctorate in education—all at the University of San Francisco. He did postdoctoral studies in psychology at Stanford University.

Hal was an award-winning teacher at San Carlos and Woodside High Schools, and an adjunct professor at his alma mater, USF. His first book, *Life's Greatest Lessons*, has sold more than a half million copies and was selected as Inspirational Book of The Year by *Writer's Digest*.

Since 1992 Dr. Urban has been passionately dedicated to the Character Education movement. He has spoken more than a thousand times in forty-four states and has made more than thirty international presentations. He speaks about good character, positive words, and good news. He gives keynote addresses, conducts workshops with educators, and talks to students of all ages. He also speaks to corporations, parents, faith groups, service organizations, and government institutions.

He has received Lifetime Achievement Awards from Character.org and the School of Education at the University of San Francisco.

Hal lives in Redwood City, California, with his wife, Cathy. His current life revolves around faith, family, friends, lifelong learning, physical fitness, sports, travel, photography, and humor.

Information about Hal's presentations and other books can be obtained in the following ways:

Website: www.halurban.com
Email: halurban@halurban.com

Dear reader,

Thank you for picking up this book and welcome to the worldwide BK community! You're joining a special group of people who have come together to create positive change in their lives, organizations, and communities.

## What's BK all about?

Our mission is to connect people and ideas to create a world that works for all.

Why? Our communities, organizations, and lives get bogged down by old paradigms of self-interest, exclusion, hierarchy, and privilege. But we believe that can change. That's why we seek the leading experts on these challenges—and share their actionable ideas with you.

## A welcome gift

To help you get started, we'd like to offer you a **free copy** of one of our bestselling ebooks:

**www.bkconnection.com/welcome**

When you claim your **free ebook**, you'll also be subscribed to our blog.

## Our freshest insights

Access the best new tools and ideas for leaders at all levels on our blog at ideas.bkconnection.com.

Sincerely,

Your friends at Berrett-Koehler

Certified

Corporation